Primary Language Arts
Grade 5

NSC Edition

Daphne Paizee,
Catherine Casey,
Mitzie-Ann Jackson

The Publishers would like to thank the following for permission to reproduce copyright material.

Text credits

p.24: © 'The Machine' by Lorraine Craik; p.75: © 'Being a tree' by Opal Palmer Adisa; p.98 & p.228: © Dreamer: Saving Our Wild World by Brian Moses, published by Otter-Barry Books, 2018; p.126: © John Lyons. All rights reserved.; p.134: © 'Fruits' by Opal Palmer Adisa; p.232: © Headline from The Gleaner.

Photo credits

t = top, b = below, l = left, r = right, c = centre, b/g = background

p.8: (tl) © Rawpixel.com/stock.adobe.com, (tc) © Fxquadro/stock.adobe.com, (tr) © zhu difeng/stock.adobe.com, (bl) © Kadmy/stock.adobe.com, (bc) © ihorvsn/stock.adobe.com, (br) © Paolese/stock.adobe.com; p.9: © mipan/stock.adobe.com, © Sergii Moscaliuk/stock.adobe.com, © Oleg/stock.adobe.com, © koosen/stock.adobe.com, © Mikhail/stock.adobe.com, © WDnet Studio/stock.adobe.com, © DenisProduction.com/stock.adobe.com; p.10: (l) © dimedrol68/stock.adobe.com, (cl) © Wire_man/stock.adobe.com, (cr) © Adomo/stock.adobe.com, (r) © BlureArt/stock.adobe.com; p.15: (t) © Africa Studio/stock.adobe.com, (b) © Vadim/stock.adobe.com; p.20: © Oleksandr/stock.adobe.com; p.21: © Sailorr/stock.adobe.com; p.22: © Andrey Popov/stock.adobe.com; p.34: © venusangel/stock.adobe.com; p.38: (tl) © monticelllllo/stock.adobe.com, (tr) © ValentinValkov/stock.adobe.com, (bl) © Shawn Hempel/stock.adobe.com, (br) © BlureArt/stock.adobe.com; p.39: (l) © diy13/stock.adobe.com, (cl) © gonzalocalle/stock.adobe.com, (cr) © New Africa/stock.adobe.com, (r) © Dmitry_Evs/stock.adobe.com; p.47: © Alexey Zarodov/stock.adobe.com, © vitalliy/stock.adobe.com, © Pixel-Shot/stock.adobe.com, © New Africa/stock.adobe.com, © Click98/stock.adobe.com, © didecs/stock.adobe.com, © thanksforbuying/stock.adobe.com; p.49: © Everett Collection/Alamy.com; p.50: © LIGHTFIELD STUDIOS/stock.adobe.com; p.53: (t) © MAXSHOT_PL/stock.adobe.com, © Ruslan Gilmanshin/stock.adobe.com, © REPORT/Shutterstock.com, (b) © Denis Rozhnovsky/stock.adobe.com, © Gabriela/stock.adobe.com, © tarasov_vl/stock.adobe.com, © Andrey Popov/stock.adobe.com, © Scanrail/stock.adobe.com, © Cobalt/stock.adobe.com; p.55: © Gabriela/stock.adobe.com, © Cobalt/stock.adobe.com, © Denis Rozhnovsky/stock.adobe.com, © Scanrail/stock.adobe.com; p.58: (t) © Sergey Peterman/stock.adobe.com, © Sergey Peterman/stock.adobe.com, © Karen Roach/stock.adobe.com, © Denis Rozhnovsky/stock.adobe.com, (b) © Tiler84/stock.adobe.com, © BillionPhotos.com/stock.adobe.com, © Scanrail/stock.adobe.com, © Cobalt/stock.adobe.com; p.63: (tl) © stockphoto-graf/stock.adobe.com, (tc) © Paul Bodea/stock.adobe.com, (tr) © Destina/stock.adobe.com, (b) © Stalvalki/stock.adobe.com; p.64: (tl) © Sergii Moscaliuk/stock.adobe.com, (tc) © WDnet Studio/stock.adobe.com, (tr) © BlureArt/stock.adobe.com, (bl) © Sergey Peterman/stock.adobe.com, (bc) © BlureArt/stock.adobe.com, (br) © selensergen/stock.adobe.com; p.67: © Shawn Hempel/stock.adobe.com; p.80: © PhotoSpirit/stock.adobe.com; p.82: © Gian/stock.adobe.com, © Lukas/stock.adobe.com, © hin255/stock.adobe.com, © Ozkan Ozmen/stock.adobe.com, © giedriius/stock.adobe.com, (b) © kuritafsheen/stock.adobe.com, © Jennifer/stock.adobe.com, © EcoView/stock.adobe.com, © Chiragsinh/stock.adobe.com, © ondrejprosicky/stock.adobe.com; p.85: © Tarpan/stock.adobe.com; p.86: (tl) © Tarpan/stock.adobe.com, (tr) © Silver/stock.adobe.com, (cl) © Shaun/stock.adobe.com, (cr) © Tarpan/stock.adobe.com, (b) © Daniel/stock.adobe.com; p.87: © pwollinga/stock.adobe.com; p.89: (l) © Greg Meland/stock.adobe.com, (r) © andriislonchak/stock.adobe.com; p.94: (t) © supattra/stock.adobe.com, (b) © Tania Piñeiro Cordero/Wirestock Creators/stock.adobe.com; p.100: © aryfahmed/stock.adobe.com; p.109: (l) © jerzy/stock.adobe.com, (r) © Uwe Bergwitz/stock.adobe.com; p.115: © EcoView/stock.adobe.com; p.118: © Анастасия Смирнова/stock.adobe.com; p.121: (l) © panaramka/stock.adobe.com, (c) © Richard Carey/stock.adobe.com, (r) © Greg Brave/stock.adobe.com; p.124: (l) © mattcuda/stock.adobe.com, (r) © schankz/stock.adobe.com; p.126: © paul_brighton/stock.adobe.com; p.129: © Olga Gorchichko/stock.adobe.com; p.131: (t) © Tim UR/stock.adobe.com, (b) © piyaset/stock.adobe.com; p.134: © Alexander Raths/stock.adobe.com; p.144: (l) © Jacek Chabraszewski/stock.adobe.com, (r) © timolina/stock.adobe.com; p.147: © volff/stock.adobe.com, © Pixel-Shot/stock.adobe.com, © T.Lagerwall/stock.adobe.com, © Liliya Trott/stock.adobe.com, © exclusive-design/stock.adobe.com; p.170: (c) © LIGHTFIELD STUDIOS/stock.adobe.com, (b) © Art_Photo/stock.adobe.com; p.171: © Jacob Lund/stock.adobe.com; p.178: © Sergey Kamshylin/stock.adobe.com; p.179: © Iryna Volina/stock.adobe.com; p.182: © Konstantin Kulikov/stock.adobe.com; p.186: (tl) © Andrey Popov/stock.adobe.com, (tr) © Sergii/stock.adobe.com, (bl) © jetcityimage/stock.adobe.com, (br) © Ayla Harbich/stock.adobe.com; p.193: © Jimmy Tudeschi/stock.adobe.com; p.204: © Genya/stock.adobe.com; p.209: (l) © gonzagon/stock.adobe.com, (r) © spotmatikphoto/stock.adobe.com; p.217: © Krakenimages.com/stock.adobe.com; p.225: (tl) © overcrew/stock.adobe.com, (tr) © Jouni/stock.adobe.com, (b) © ronedya/stock.adobe.com; p.226: © gudkovandrey/stock.adobe.com; p.232: (l) © panaramka/stock.adobe.com; p.235: © Igor Groshev/stock.adobe.com; p.235: © Tomasz Bidermann/stock.adobe.com; p.239: © DisobeyArt/stock.adobe.com; p.241: © R. Gino Santa Maria/stock.adobe.com, (tr) © Ivan/stock.adobe.com, (bl) © wavebreak3/stock.adobe.com, (br) © JuYochi/stock.adobe.com; p.243: © Debbie Ann Powell/Shutterstock.com; p.246: (l) © kamilpetran/stock.adobe.com, (r) © kichigin19/stock.adobe.com; p.249: (t) © Archivist/stock.adobe.com, (b) © Kim Warden/stock.adobe.com; p.260: © Victoria Sharratt/stock.adobe.com.

Although every effort has been made to ensure that website addresses are correct at time of going to press, Hodder Education cannot be held responsible for the content of any website mentioned in this book. It is sometimes possible to find a relocated web page by typing in the address of the home page for a website in the URL window of your browser.

Hachette UK's policy is to use papers that are natural, renewable and recyclable products and made from wood grown in well-managed forests and other controlled sources. The logging and manufacturing processes are expected to conform to the environmental regulations of the country of origin.

To order, please visit www.hoddereducation.com or contact Customer Service at education@hachette.co.uk / +44 (0)1235 827827.

ISBN: 9781398356290

© Daphne Paizee, Catherine Casey, Mitzie-Ann Jackson and Hodder & Stoughton Limited 2024

This edition published in 2024 by

Hodder Education,

An Hachette UK Company

Carmelite House

50 Victoria Embankment

London EC4Y 0DZ

www.hoddereducation.com

Impression number 10 9 8 7 6 5 4 3 2 1

Year 2027 2026 2025 2024

All rights reserved. Apart from any use permitted under UK copyright law, no part of this publication may be reproduced or transmitted in any form or by any means, electronic or mechanical, including photocopying and recording, or held within any information storage and retrieval system, without permission in writing from the publisher or under licence from the Copyright Licensing Agency Limited. Further details of such licences (for reprographic reproduction) may be obtained from the Copyright Licensing Agency Limited, www.cla.co.uk

Cover illustration by Heather Clarke c/o D'Avila Illustration Agency.

Illustrations by Jane Commin, Claudia Eckard, Samantha van Riet and Hyphen S.A.

Typeset by Hyphen S.A.

Printed in Spain

A catalogue record for this title is available from the British Library.

MIX
Paper | Supporting responsible forestry
FSC
www.fsc.org
FSC™ C104740

Contents

Contents 3

Term 1 **Unit 1**

Energy and matter

Project 1: Machines around us 8

Speaking and listening: Jamaican Creole and Standard Jamaican English; give verbal descriptions; listen to recount information; plan and give a verbal presentation 8

Word builder: Vocabulary about machines; compound words; sight vocabulary 11

Let's read: Read a non-fiction information text; understand text structure and organisation; understand the author's purpose; build strengths in reading 15

Grammar builder: Transition words; complete sentences 17

Let's write: Plan and write in paragraphs using subheadings and topic sentences 18

Project 2: What a noise! 20

Speaking and listening: Discuss and recite a poem using rhythm and actions; Jamaican Creole and Standard Jamaican English 20

Word builder: Vocabulary about machinery and sounds; onomatopoeic words; design and play word games 22

Let's read: Read a story; summarise and sequence; comprehension skills; build strengths in reading 24

Grammar builder: Subject and predicate 26

Let's write: Plan and write a story using a visual stimulus 28

Project 3: How it works 30

Speaking and listening: Discuss and share information; describe a bicycle from a picture and explain how it works 30

Word builder: Play a word game with different vocabulary; list words by meaning; prefixes 32

Let's read: Read and rewrite an advertisement; sequence text 34

Grammar builder: Subjects, predicates and verbs; sentence construction 36

Let's write: Plan and write a set of instructions using a flow chart 37

Project 4: Machines rule! 39

Speaking and listening: Give verbal instructions; demonstrate how to use a simple machine 39

Word builder: Vocabulary about machines; definitions; suffixes 41

Let's read: Use pictures to predict; read a comic strip story; comprehension; express and justify a view 43

Grammar builder: Interjections 45

Let's write: Onomatopoeia; plan and write a story about a machine 47

Project 5: The first computers 49

Speaking and listening: Describe a picture; discuss ideas; present to class 49

Word builder: Vocabulary about computers; use word structures in understanding and spelling 51

Let's read: Read an information text; identify main ideas; identify purpose and features of text types 53

Grammar builder: Subject; adjectives; nouns; sentence construction 56

Let's write: Plan and write an information text 58

Project 6: Imaginary machines! 60

Speaking and listening: Describe a real and an imaginary machine 60

Word builder: Compound words; word families; strategies for identifying unknown words 62

Let's read: Read a poem; discuss and answer questions; spelling patterns and rhymes; draw a comic strip of the poem 65

Grammar builder: Subjects; predicates; interjections 67

Let's write: Draw and label an imaginary machine; onomatopoeia; plan and write a poem 68

Term 1 Unit 1 Review and assessment 69

Term 1 Unit 2
Diversity, sustainability and interdependence

Project 7: My world 72
- **Speaking and listening:** Class discussion; look and listen outdoors; make a presentation 72
- **Word builder:** Vocabulary about sights and sounds around us; alphabetical order; use a dictionary 74
- **Let's read:** Read a poem and act it out; similes and metaphors; compare poetry with other forms of text 75
- **Grammar builder:** Punctuation 78
- **Let's write:** Read and write an acrostic poem about the environment 79

Project 8: Different places, different experiences 81
- **Speaking and listening:** Use Jamaican Creole and Standard Jamaican English 81
- **Word builder:** Vocabulary about animals from different habitats; letter clusters; use a dictionary 82
- **Let's read:** Read a diary; compare information in two texts 85
- **Grammar builder:** Connecting words; conjunctions 88
- **Let's write:** Plan and write paragraphs about an imaginary trip 89

Project 9: What is the impact on the environment? 90
- **Speaking and listening:** Discuss and answer questions on a set of pictures; prepare and give a presentation 90
- **Word builder:** Vocabulary about the environment; syllables; use context clues; root words, prefixes and suffixes 92
- **Let's read:** Read an information text; locate main ideas; identify positive and negative statements 94
- **Grammar builder:** Verbs in past, present and future tense 96
- **Let's write:** Plan and write an essay on a given topic 97

Project 10: Our natural resources 98
- **Speaking and listening:** Discuss and read a poem aloud; listen to recall information; prepare and deliver a presentation 98
- **Word builder:** Vocabulary about the environment; strategies for understanding new words; understand and use words in context 100
- **Let's read:** Read non-fiction books; use contents pages; locate information in a book; use a glossary and an index 101
- **Grammar builder:** Use adverbs in your writing 104
- **Let's write:** Plan and write a contents list for a book 105

Project 11: Where are the wetlands? 106
- **Speaking and listening:** Discuss a map; listen to recall information; prepare and deliver a presentation; express and justify a point of view 106
- **Word builder:** Vocabulary about wetlands; using a dictionary; create a word puzzle; write a definition 108
- **Let's read:** Read a map; read a report; understand different features in text 109
- **Grammar builder:** Direct speech; reported speech 111
- **Let's write:** Plan and write an information text in paragraphs, use subheadings; draft and use a checklist for editing and improving writing 113

Project 12: Which animals live in the grasslands? 115
- **Speaking and listening:** Class discussion; listen to and read aloud a poem; prepare and deliver a presentation 115
- **Word builder:** Vocabulary about animals and grassland; strategies for reading and understanding an unknown word; make a glossary 117
- **Let's read:** Read a magazine article including headings and subheadings; use information from the article; understand the purpose of the article 118
- **Grammar builder:** Noun phrases 120
- **Let's write:** Plan and write a story, including characters, setting, problem, resolution, ending 121

Term 1 Unit 2 Review and assessment 123

Term 2 Unit 1
Health and well-being; nutrition

Project 13: Special food 126

Speaking and listening: Listen to and read a poem aloud; compare Jamaican Creole with Standard Jamaican English 126

Word builder: Vocabulary about baking; syllables; spelling; silent letters 127

Let's read: Read about favourite foods; comprehension questions 129

Grammar builder: Use adverbs 130

Let's write: Use similes and metaphors in writing poems about food; use a writing frame 131

Project 14: At the market 134

Speaking and listening: Listen to and read a poem aloud; discuss with a partner; make a word puzzle using adjectives 134

Word builder: Vocabulary about fruits; alphabetical order; strategies for reading unfamiliar words 136

Let's read: Locate information in a text; read a playscript; compare a playscript with prose fiction; summarise; read with expression 137

Grammar builder: Direct speech; reported speech 140

Let's write: Plan and write a playscript 142

Project 15: Healthy choices 144

Speaking and listening: Listen respectfully; hold a class debate 144

Word builder: Vocabulary about food and health; strategies for reading unfamiliar words; mnemonics 145

Let's read: Read a report; comprehension questions 147

Grammar builder: Change the meaning of sentences; change positive and negative sentences 149

Let's write: Plan and write a story; use a story map; identify the title, characters, setting, problem, resolution and ending; use adjectives, adverbs, similes and metaphors 150

Project 16: Do advertisements persuade us? 152

Speaking and listening: Listen and respond to an advertisement; prepare and give a presentation evaluating an advertisement 152

Word builder: Vocabulary of food adjectives; word endings; superlatives; persuasive words 153

Let's read: Read, compare and evaluate different advertisements 154

Grammar builder: Prepositions of time 156

Let's write: Plan and write a persuasive advertisement 157

Project 17: Food labels 159

Speaking and listening: Phrases used in canteens and restaurants; use Jamaican Creole and Standard Jamaican English; role play visiting a canteen or restaurant 159

Word builder: Vocabulary related to food packaging; use a dictionary; prefixes 160

Let's read: Read food packaging; identify and locate specific information; persuasive writing 162

Grammar builder: Subject-verb agreement ... 164

Let's write: Write a formal letter; plan an event; write an invitation 165

Project 18: Careers around food 167

Speaking and listening: Read an interview aloud; perform a role play following the interview script; plan questions for an interview and role play it 167

Word builder: Vocabulary related to careers around food; suffixes; definitions 168

Let's read: Skim and scan; locate specific information; predict; summarise 170

Grammar builder: Intervening phrases 172

Let's write: Research a job connected with food; write a structured report in paragraphs; mind map; subheadings; topic sentences; adjectives and adverbs; intervening sentences; self-review and evaluation 173

Term 2 Unit 1 Review and assessment 174

Term 2 Unit 2
Institutions and parish decisions

Project 19: Parishes in Jamaica 178

Speaking and listening: Class/group discussion; look at and compare maps, talk about locality 178

Word builder: Vocabulary about Jamaican history and geography; use dictionaries; write own definitions; synonyms; antonyms 180

5

Let's read: Skim and scan for general comprehension and to locate specific information 182

Grammar builder: Transitional words............... 184

Let's write: Research, plan and write an information text; identify key facts.................... 185

Project 20: The roles and functions of the parish council 186

Speaking and listening: Describe pictures; discussion; ask questions; conduct interviews 186

Word builder: Vocabulary relating to parish services; digraphs, trigraphs, blends and clusters 188

Let's read: Read non-fiction texts; headings, subheadings, signal words and phrases, diagrams, photographs and captions................ 190

Grammar builder: Pronouns................................ 191

Let's write: Research, plan and write a text introducing the local Mayor to your school......192

Project 21: Making changes......................193

Speaking and listening: Read a playscript aloud; prepare and act out a role play...............193

Word builder: Vocabulary about local services; compound words................................. 194

Let's read: Read a letter; skim and scan for general comprehension and to locate specific information; express and justify your response to a piece of writing 195

Grammar builder: Subject-verb agreement; past and present tense............................... 197

Let's write: Write a formal letter; persuasive writing; give feedback 199

Project 22: Parish councils in the news ... 201

Speaking and listening: Prepare and conduct a class debate............................. 201

Word builder: Morphemes 202

Let's read: Read newspaper articles; read headlines; comprehension questions................. 203

Grammar builder: Linking ideas and sentences; sequencing words........................ 205

Let's write: Research, plan and write a news report; write a headline 206

Project 23: Rules and regulations............. 208

Speaking and listening: Read and discuss old by-laws; debate opinions; identify pros and cons; make a class presentation................. 208

Word builder: Vocabulary around rules and regulations; word games; words with multiple meanings.. 210

Let's read: Read newspaper reports; summarise text; infer information from text.. 211

Grammar builder: Apostrophes of possession and contraction 212

Let's write: Write a formal letter; write a letter of complaint... 213

Project 24: Local governments in other Caribbean countries....................................214

Speaking and listening: Identify and discuss speaking and listening skills; work in groups to create a poster or presentation 214

Word builder: Vocabulary around administration and government; nouns; segmenting words into individual sounds........ 215

Let's read: Prior knowledge; read a table; use information to make comparisons; research local government in another country 217

Grammar builder: Punctuate paragraphs....... 219

Let's write: Research, plan and write information text in paragraphs........................... 220

Term 2 Unit 2 Review and assessment ... 222

Term 3   Unit 1

Living things and life processes

Project 25: Pollution.................................... 225

Speaking and listening: Discuss information in photographs; use question words to devise questions about pictures 225

Word builder: Vocabulary about pollution; synonyms; use a thesaurus.................................. 227

Let's read: Listen to and read a poem; discuss and answer questions; translate text into Jamaican Creole; identify personification; express and justify response to text 228

Grammar builder: Revise regular and irregular verb tenses; convert between verb tenses... 230

Let's write: Similes; metaphors; onomatopoeia; personification; write a poem or song on a given theme 231

Project 26: Collecting information 232

Speaking and listening: Read and discuss information texts; devise a survey; ask and answer questions 232

Word builder: Vocabulary around air pollution; identify word families and parts of speech; use words in context; use a dictionary 234

Let's read: Skim text for general comprehension; read to locate specific information; make notes of the main ideas 235

Grammar builder: Collective nouns 237

Let's write: Plan and write a factual report; use own research; write a bibliography 238

Project 27: Protest against pollution 239

Speaking and listening: Read and discuss slogans; express and justify an opinion; discuss and role play 239

Word builder: Vocabulary about pollution; solve anagrams; complete sentences 241

Let's read: Skim and read a newspaper article; summarise main ideas; role play an article 243

Grammar builder: Use quotation marks 244

Let's write: Design and make a poster warning about air pollution 245

Project 28: Pollution and progress 246

Speaking and listening: Hold a debate for and against a motion 246

Word builder: Vocabulary around pollution and progress; use a dictionary; make sentences; homophones; homonyms 247

Let's read: Read captions; read title; read text; share ideas; summarise 249

Grammar builder: Present and past tense; use correct tense in writing 251

Let's write: Draft and write an informal letter or email expressing a point of view 252

Project 29: Burning fossil fuels 253

Speaking and listening: Make notes while listening to a non-fiction text and a poem; locate the main facts; identify how the text made you feel; summarise 253

Word builder: Vocabulary around fossil fuels; match words with definitions; syllabification; mnemonics/spelling strategies 254

Let's read: Skim text for general comprehension, scan to locate specific information; read a pie chart 256

Grammar builder: Pronouns 258

Let's write: Discuss similarities and differences between different text types; identify style, features and layouts; compare two pieces of writing on the same subject 259

Project 30: Clean air 260

Speaking and listening: Ask and answer questions; research and discuss facts, data, charts and photographs; prepare a presentation 260

Word builder: Vocabulary around air and pollution; antonyms; synonyms; play a word game 261

Let's read: Skim a graphic story; discuss the story; ask and answer questions; devise a title for the story; plot the story on a diagram or chart 263

Grammar builder: Present continuous tense; present simple tense; past tense 265

Let's write: Plan and write a story; characters, setting, plot structure, title, direct speech; edit and review 266

Term 3 Unit 1 Review and assessment 267

TERM 1

Unit 1

Project 1

Speaking and listening

1. Spend two minutes thinking about all the machines that you have already used today and discuss with your partner. Who has used more?

2. Now look at the photographs of different machines that we use and discuss the questions below. Can you guess what each machine does?

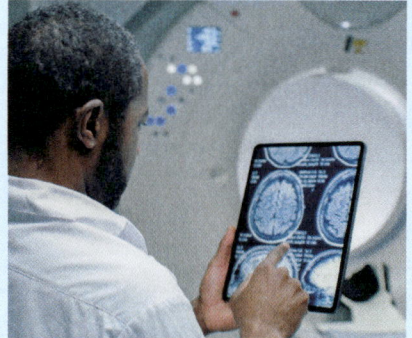

- Tell your partner what clues in the photograph have helped you.
- Do you know the names of any of these machines?
- If you do not know the name of the machine, can you make up a name that helps to explain what the machine does?

Project 1 – Machines around us

3 Pick a machine word from the bag your teacher has prepared. Describe the machine to a group. Can the group guess which machine you are describing? Remember, don't say the name!

4 Choose a Jamaican Creole (JC) phrase about machines and translate it into Standard Jamaican English (SJE). Your teacher may have prepared some for you. What is the same and what is different about the phrases?

5 With your partner, prepare a short presentation about a machine you use at home or at school. Present information about your chosen machine to the class:

- What does it look like?
- What does it sound like?
- What is the purpose of the machine?
- Why is it useful?
- How does it work?

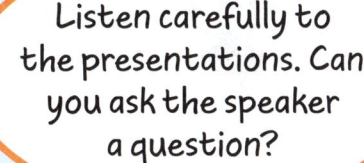

Listen carefully to the presentations. Can you ask the speaker a question?

6 Discuss with a partner how important machines are and why we use them.

- Why are machines useful?
- How do machines help us?
- Which machine could you not do without?

Term 1 Unit 1

Remember ☆☆☆

Be a good listener.
- Take turns speaking.
- Look at the person who is speaking.
- Think about what is being said.
- Ask the speaker questions.

ICT opportunity

Use the internet to research sounds made by different machines.

- Can you describe the sounds the machines above make?

 ping

 tick

 whizz

- Play a sound made by a machine and ask your partner to identify what machine is making the noise.

10

Project 1 – Machines around us

Word builder

Vocabulary box

aeroplane	fridge	microwave	taxicab
bulldozer	hairdryer	minivan	tugboat
mobile phone	kettle	railway	water pump
dishwasher	laptop	washing machine	

1 Read the words about machines in the vocabulary box above. Complete the table according to how we use the machines. Can you add more words to your lists?

Machines we use for transport	Machines we use at home

2 With your partner, identify the compound words in the vocabulary box and circle them in your table.

L👀k and learn

Compound words are made up of two words.

For example:

lap + top = laptop (a computer you can use on top of your lap)

micro + wave = microwave (a machine that works with small (micro) waves of energy)

water + pump = water pump (a machine that pumps water)

digital + camera = digital camera (a camera with a digital electronic system)

When you learn a new compound word, look carefully to see if it is written as one word or two words.

11

Term 1 Unit 1

3 Look at the words in the vocabulary box on the previous page. Write the compound words in the table and use a dictionary to find out the meaning of each compound word.

Compound word	Definition
aeroplane = aero + plane	A machine with wings that flies.

4 Make compound words that are the names of machines using the words below to help you. Write the compound words in your notebook.

aero   auto   tug   cruise
taxi   bull   mobile   plane
ship   boat   dozer   cab

Example:

aero + plane = aero plane

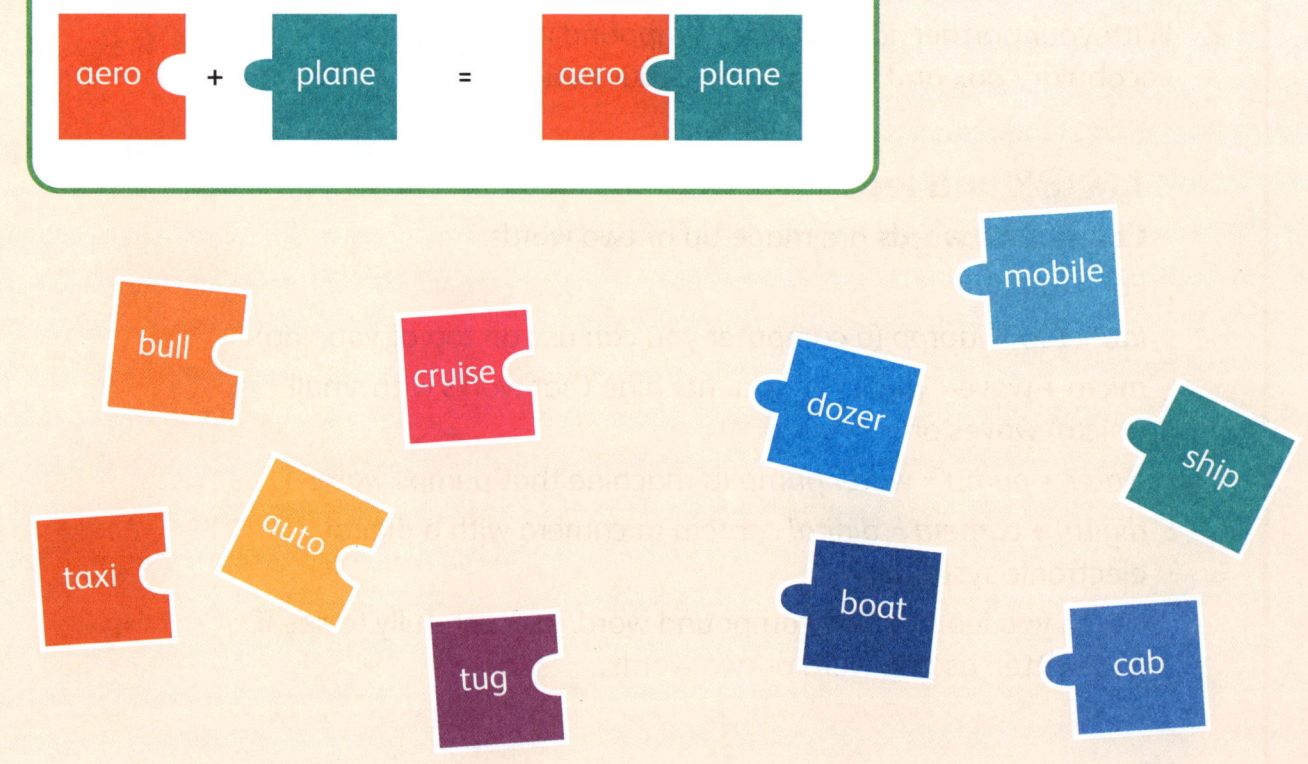

5 Read the definitions and write the compound words.

1. A machine used to dry your hair.

| h | | | | d | | | | |

2. A machine that washes dishes.

| d | | | | w | | | | | |

3. A machine used to cook food quickly.

| m | | | | | w | | | |

4. A computer you can use on your lap.

| l | | | t | | |

ICT opportunity

Use a digital dictionary or a thesaurus to find out the meaning of compound words and to research words about machines.

Look and learn

There are three different types of compound words.

- **Closed compound words** that are written as one word.

  For example: *hairdryer, dishwasher*

- **Hyphenated compound words** that are two words joined by a hyphen.

  For example: *part-time, co-worker*

- **Open compound words** that are written as two words.

  For example: *sewing machine, water pump, electric fan*

Extension task

Copy the table below in your notebook. Use the headings *Closed*, *Hyphenated* and *Open*. Sort the words in the vocabulary box according to the type of compound word. Add any more compound words you can think of.

Vocabulary box

laptop, well-known, full-time, part-time, battery-powered, crop harvester, sewing machine, microwave, aeroplane, water pump

Closed	Hyphenated	Open
laptop		

Let's read

1 Read the text carefully and discuss the following questions with a partner.

> **The importance of machines in our lives**
>
> **What are machines?**
>
> Machines make it easier to do tasks. Without machines, many tasks would take a very long time to complete or we would not be able to do them at all. Machines can be small, like a knife or a tap. Machines can also be huge, like crop harvesters.
>
> **How do machines help me at home?**
>
> Our homes are full of machines. A fridge keeps our food fresh and gives us a cold drink on a very hot day. An oven or microwave allows us to cook and heat up food quickly. Imagine if we had to light a fire every time we needed something cooked or warmed up!
>
> **Where else do we use machines?**
>
> We use machines everywhere. We take mobile phones wherever we go to send messages, surf the internet or do calculations. Without machines we would also need to walk everywhere. There would be no bicycles, cars or buses!

1. What type of text is this: a story, an informative text, a poem, instructions or a comic?

2. How can you tell what the text type is? What clues are there?

3. Can you find the following features in the text? Point them out to your partner.

   heading   subheadings   photographs

4. Why are subheadings useful? Give at least two reasons.

5. What purpose might the author have written this text for?

2 Use information from the text to answer the questions in full sentences.

1. Give two reasons why machines are important.

2. The text tells us there are huge machines, such as crop harvesters. What other words could you use instead of *huge*, without changing the meaning?

3   What does a fridge do?

4   Why would we have to walk everywhere if we did not have machines?

3 Work in pairs to find the topic sentence in each paragraph.

L👀k and learn
A **topic sentence** gives the main idea of a paragraph. The other sentences give additional information.

Research and study skills

1 Identify your strengths as a reader and one thing to improve on. Try to give examples.
  - Can you recognise lots of words by looking at them?
  - Can you decode words you don't know?
  - Can you read fluently?
  - Can you read with expression?
  - Can you identify features and organisation of different text types?
  - Can you understand what texts are saying and find information to answer questions?

2 Copy and complete the sentences in your notebook.

When I am reading, I can _____. For example, _____.

I would like to get better at _____.

When I am reading, I can do this by _____.

ICT opportunity

Find an informative text about a machine of your choice. Read the text carefully. Then answer the following questions:
- What is the purpose of the machine?
- Can you find the topic sentence in each paragraph?
- Can you find an interesting fact about the machine?

Grammar builder

Look and learn

Transition words join phrases, sentences and paragraphs together. They help our writing to flow. Here are some examples of transition words: *first, second, next, then, lastly, and, which, but, because, therefore, for, so, while, afterwards, consequently, hence, meanwhile, even though, however, or.*

1 Copy these sentences in your notebook and underline the transition words.

   1 On the way to school our unreliable car broke down, so we were late.

   2 The old vacuum cleaner was not working, therefore the rug was dirty.

   3 There was popcorn all over the floor because I forgot to put the lid on the popcorn machine properly.

   4 I typed the story on my laptop, which was much quicker than writing it.

   5 A stone broke the lawn mower, consequently I could not cut the grass.

2 Read the sentences with a partner. Choose an appropriate transition word to complete each sentence.

   1 My hair was still wet _____ the hair dryer was not working.

   2 The kettle whistled _____ the water boiled.

   3 The chain came off my bike _____ I had to stop and mend it.

   4 The toaster was turned up too high _____ the bread burnt.

   5 I forgot to charge the battery _____ my mobile phone was not working.

3 With your partner, copy these phrases onto slips of paper. Place the slips of paper into a box. Pick a phrase and read it to your partner. Can your partner use a transition word and complete the sentence? Repeat, taking it in turns with your partner to pick the phrase.

   1 The microwave was broken …

   2 Water was leaking out of the washing machine …

   3 The laptop screen had cracked …

   4 I emptied the dishwasher …

   5 I had a new shiny bike …

   6 The new vacuum cleaner sucked up my sock …

Term 1 Unit 1

Let's write

Task

Write three paragraphs to explain which machines you use in your daily life and why you use them, following the steps given below.

Plan

1. Plan your paragraphs. Think of three subheadings to organise your writing. Here are some questions that might help you:
   - What machines do you use at home?
   - Are there any machines in your school?
   - Are there any machines you would like to own?

2. Start to think about what you will include in each paragraph. Remember that you need to explain why you use the machines.

Machines I use at home:
kettle (hot water)
fridge (food)
stove
lawn mower

Machines I use at school:
computer
calculator

Machines I would like to own:
robot
motorbike

Remember ☆☆☆

The **topic sentence** gives the main idea of the paragraph. Make sure your topic sentence has at least one verb.

3. Write a topic sentence for each paragraph. Now that you have planned what you will talk about in each one, writing will be easier.

18

Write

4   Draft your paragraphs. Start with your subheadings and topic sentences and write another three sentences for each paragraph. Try to write long and short sentences. You can include questions and exclamations, too. Check your work against the "Editor's checklist".

> **Editor's checklist**
>
> When you finish your work, check it carefully.
>
> - Do all your sentences have verbs?
> - Did you use different types of sentences?
> - Did you check your spelling?
> - Do your subheadings all relate to the title?
> - Do your topic sentences introduce and summarise the paragraph?
> - Did you include questions and exclamations?
> - Did you explain why you used the machines?

Evaluate

5   Now swap your work with your partner and check his or her work against the checklist. Take turns to explain what you liked about each other's writing. If you think your partner has missed something from the checklist, explain how they could improve. Make sure your comments are positive and clear.

6   Write two things you did well in your writing and give an example for each. Then write down what you would like to improve in your next piece of writing and how you will achieve this.

ICT opportunity

Write about and discuss useful machines at home and at school in a class blog. What machines would you like to use in the future?

Term 1 Unit 1

Project 2

Speaking and listening

1. Discuss with your partner. What do you know about trains? How many times have you been in a train? How would you describe what they sound like?

2. Listen as your teacher reads this poem. Clap to the rhythm as you listen. Do you think it sounds like a train?

Song of the train

Clickety-clack,
Wheels on the track,
This is the way
They begin the attack:
Click-ety-clack,
Click-ety-clack,
Click-ety, *clack-ety*,
Click-ety
Clack.

Clickety-clack,
Over the crack,
Faster and faster

The song of the track:
Click-ety-clack,
Click-ety-clack,
Click-ety, clack-ety,
Clack-ety
Clack.

Riding in front,
Riding in back,
Everyone hears
The song of the track:
Click-ety-clack,
Click-ety-clack,

Click-ety, *click-ety*,
Clack-ety
Clack.

by David McCord

3. To create rhythm, this poem uses words that rhyme. How many words can you find that rhyme with *clack*? What other words can you think of that rhyme with *clack*?

4. Work in groups. Recite and role play the poem with rhythm. Work together to make it sound as much like a train as possible, using only the words from the poem.

Remember ☆☆☆

Words that **rhyme** end in the same sounds.
The **rhythm** is the beat of the poem which is made by repeating sound patterns.

Project 2 – What a noise!

ICT opportunity

Use ICT tools to record and edit your group reciting and presenting this poem. You can either record video or sound.

5. Listen to the recording of your group reciting the poem and evaluate your performance. Discuss with your group.
   - Did you speak clearly and loudly enough?
   - Did you speak with rhythm?
   - Was your performance fluent?
   - Did you use proper expressions?
   - What could you improve?

6. Think again about how you described the train's sounds at the beginning. Do you think the train in the poem sounds the same as the train you described? Write a sentence to describe how your train sounds.

7. Work with a partner. Write common Jamaican Creole (JC) phrases about trains and translate to Standard Jamaican English (SJE). Can you use words that describe the sound of the train?

Did you know that Jamaica has the third oldest railway system in the Americas, which connects all the ports on the island?

Term 1 Unit 1

Word builder

Vocabulary box

cowered	groans	metal	terrified
crackled	hesitated	moans	thunderous
crate	jumbled	nobody	track
creaked	menacing	railway	twisted
everyone			

1 Read all the words in the vocabulary box. Write three column headings in your notebook: *Word*, *Meaning* and *Sentence*. Copy the words into the first column. Fill in the meanings in the second column for the words you know. Are there any you can guess? Write these meanings, too, and check them in a dictionary. In the last column, write sentences with these words.

Look and learn

When we use **words that imitate sounds**, we are using **onomatopoeia** – it is pronounced as "on-oh-mat-o-pee-ya". For example: *The door <u>creaked</u> open.*

We often use **exclamations** with words like these, too.
For example: *pop! clang! hmm! ping! beep! bang! click! squeak!*

Example:
The microwave finished with a ping!

> **Vocabulary box**
>
> pop   clank   ping   beep   bang   click   squeak

2. Read aloud the sound words in the vocabulary box. What machine sounds could you describe with these words? Can you add three more words to the list in your notebook? Write down a sentence for each new word.

3. With your partner, play a word game.
   - Write each word in the vocabulary box onto two individual cards to make two sets which are the same.
   - Mix the cards up.
   - Spread the cards face down on the table.
   - Take turns with your partner to turn over two cards and read the words aloud.
   - If the two cards match, you keep the cards. If they do not match, turn the cards back over.
   - Then it is your partner's turn.
   - Repeat until all the cards are gone.

   Who has collected the most cards?

4. Work with a partner or in a small group and design a game to learn and practise sight words.
   - Choose 10–15 words about machines to practise.
   - What resources will you need? Collect and create the resources (cards/dice/pencil and paper).
   - Write instructions for your game.
   - Practise your game and teach the class your game.

Let's read

1 What type of text is this? How do you know? What features can you identify?

The Machine

The menacing metal machine creaked and crackled as one claw-like arm stretched out in the direction of the terrified twins.

Shanice and Sean cowered in fear and tried to back away, but there was a pile of wooden crates behind them.

"O dear! Doan mean to frighten you!" came from somewhere deep inside the twisted metal hulk, and there was a clunk and a clatter as a piece of metal fell to the concrete floor.

"Wow! It can talk!" exclaimed Sean.

As they watched, the machine rose up on unsteady metal legs, and loomed above them. The twins were still afraid. Tinny music began to come out of the machine. It began to dance, in a slow, stiff, serious sort of way. Then, with a tremendous, thunderous crash, it fell over.

"O dear! O dear! Mi need to fix! P'ease elp!"

Sean and Shanice rushed over to the heap of jumbled, metal limbs and body parts and hesitated, unsure what to do to help.

"Take his hand that side, let's try and get him on his feet", suggested Shanice, and the twins heaved at his arms. There were creaks and groans and moans and the sound of metal grinding on metal, until, with a rusty howl, the metal machine was on its feet.

"T'ank yu, t'ank yu!" he said, as the twins stepped back, still a little nervous of the huge hulk. They looked up at his metal face high above them.

"Need sum oil!" he declared. So, with a twin holding each of his huge metal hands, they set off in search of some oil.

by Lorraine Craik

2 Discuss and answer these questions about the story.

1. What did Sean and Shanice see?

2. What did the machine say? Say it in Jamaican Creole (JC) and in Standard Jamaican English (SJE).

3. How did the twins feel when they first saw the machine? Find words in the story that tell us how they felt.

4. Was the robot friendly, or unfriendly? Explain two ways that you know.

5. Did you enjoy the story? Did it make you laugh? What did you like/dislike about it?

6. What is the purpose of this text? To inform, entertain or persuade?

7. As a class, make a summary of events in the order in which they happen in the story. Two events have been added to help you:

| The machine reaches for the twins. They are scared. | → | | → | The machine stands up and falls over again. | → | |

3 Role play the story to the class in groups of three. Choose two different times in the story to "freeze" in position. Each person should say one sentence about each of the following:

- what your character is feeling and thinking at that moment
- how you know that from the story.

Research and study skills

Think about the text that you just read. Imagine you were trying to explain to a Grade 1 student how you found the answers to the questions about the text. What would you tell them?

Grammar builder

Look and learn

Sentences have two parts, a **subject** and a **predicate**.
The **subject** is what or whom the sentence is about.
It can be a noun or a pronoun.
The **predicate** tells us about the subject.
It always has a verb and can be one word or a group of words.
For example:

She runs.
The old robot terrified the twins.
Clarice and Charlie cowered in fear.
They set off in search of some oil.
I have a headache.

1. Copy the table into your notebook. Put the subject in the first column and the predicate in the second column. Here is an example:

Subject	Predicate
Machines	are very useful.

   1. Trains move along railway lines.
   2. This class is very noisy!
   3. The wheels of the train go *clickety-clack*.
   4. "It can talk!"

2. Read the story in the "Let's read" lesson again. Find the subjects of these sentences.

   1. _____ rose up on unsteady metal legs.
   2. _____ were still afraid.
   3. _____ rushed over to the heap of jumbled, metal limbs.
   4. _____ looked up at his metal face high above them.

3   Unscramble these words to make sentences that are grammatically correct. Start with the subjects. Each sentence should start with a capital letter and end with a full stop or an exclamation.

1   two cars we have

    _____

2   frightened the twins the robot

    _____

3   my father a new television bought

    _____

4   a new mobile phone Tyrone has

    _____

ICT opportunity

Choose a machine to research. Find a short information text about your chosen machine. Print off the text.
Work with a partner to underline the subject in each sentence.

Let's write

Task

Look at the picture. You are going to write a story about this machine. Follow these steps.

Plan

1. Think of some words you could use to describe this machine. Write your words in a mind map. Here are some questions to help you:

   • What has happened to the machine?

   • Can the machine speak?

   • How does it sound? List as many words that describe the sound of the machine as you can. Can you use onomatopoeic words?

   • Do you want your readers to be scared or excited, or do you want them to laugh?

Remember ☆☆☆

Onomatopoeic words sound like the word they are describing.
For example: *buzz, bang, crack, zap, whizz*

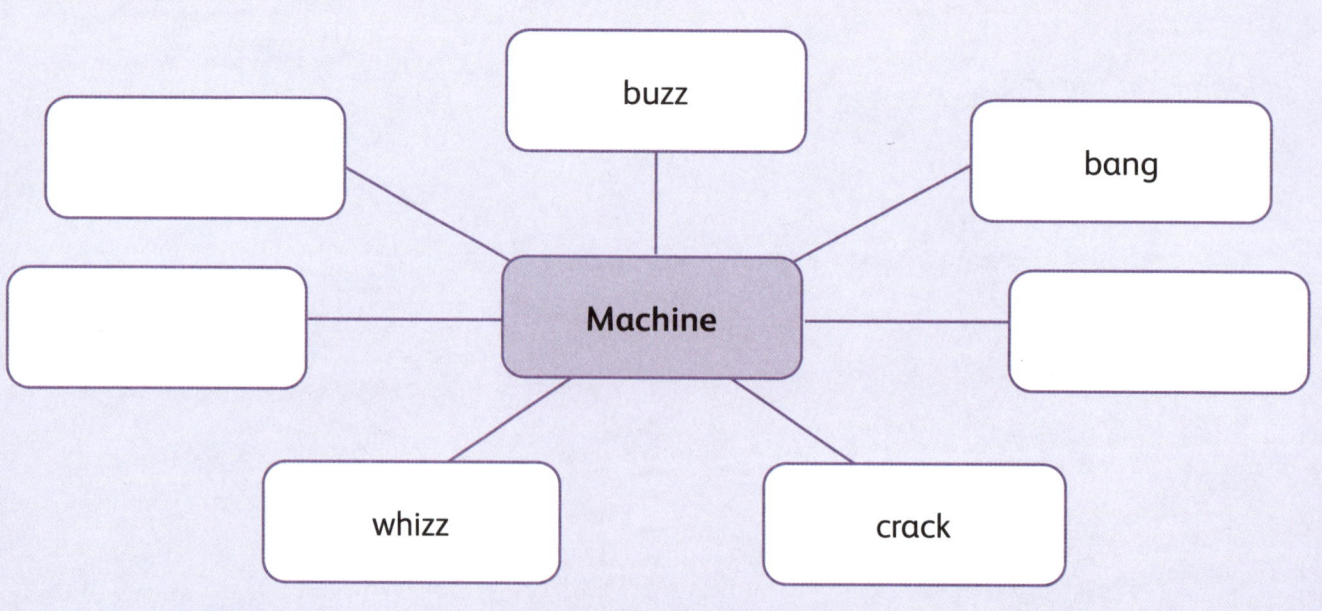

2. Make up a story about the machine. You could draw a flow chart like this:

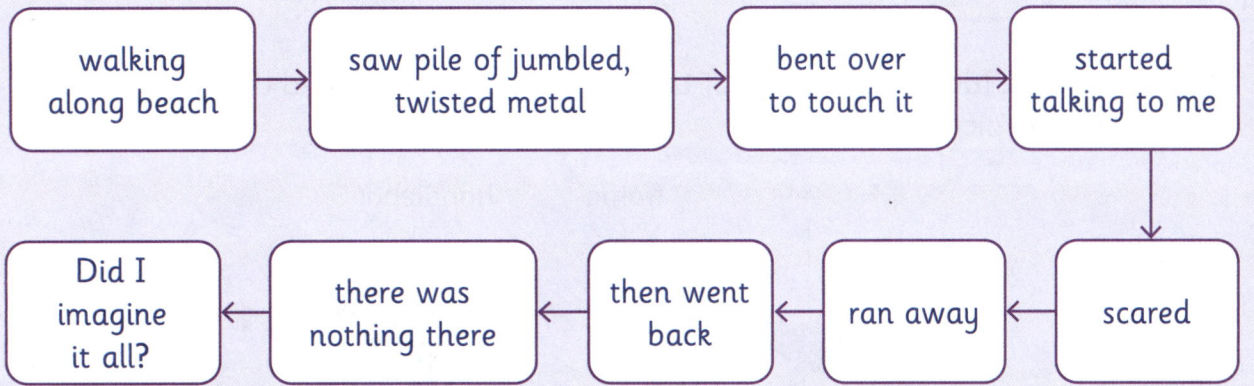

Write

3. Write a draft of your story. Try to use sound words in your story. Think about whether your machine is exciting, funny or scary. Choose words to describe it that make the person reading it feel the same way about the machine as you do.

4. Use the "Editor's checklist" to edit and improve your story.

Editor's checklist

When you finish your work, check it carefully.
- Did you describe the machine?
- Is the sequence of events clear in the story?
- Did you use sound words?
- Did you check your spelling?

Evaluate

5. Work in small groups. Take turns to read your stories aloud to your group with expression. Ask each member of the group to write down one word which describes how they felt about the story, for example: *excited, amused, scared*.

There are no right or wrong answers, but the answers will help you understand if your listeners felt the same way as you do about the story.

6. Write in your notebook two things you did well in your writing and give an example for each. Then write down what you would like to improve in your next piece of writing and how you will achieve this.

Project 3

Speaking and listening

1. Work in pairs. Identify the parts of the bicycle by reading aloud the labels on the picture.

2. In your notebook, match the parts of the bicycle to the functions of each part.

Part	Function
frame	helps the rider to balance and exert force to pedal
handlebar	makes the bicycle move forward
chain	controls the movement and allows you to stop or slow down
pedal	turns the wheels when you pedal
wheel	holds the parts together
brake	can increase the speed and power at which you pedal because it is linked to the chain
gear	makes the chain move around

3 Use the information in the table to explain to your partner how a bicycle works. Discuss with each other what would happen if:
- the chain was missing
- the handlebars were missing
- the brakes were missing.

A bicycle is a complex machine made up of smaller machines!

4 Work with a partner to write common Jamaican Creole (JC) phrases about bicycles or bicycle parts. Translate the phrases into Standard Jamaican English (SJE).

ICT opportunity

Watch short video clips about bicycles, such as how to mend a puncture or how a bicycle is made. Discuss the video clips with a partner. Listen out for the bicycle parts and their functions.

Word builder

Vocabulary box

add	healthy	monocycle	switch on
amazing	in a jiffy	peel	television
bicycle	juice	pop in	tricycle
extra	leave	switch off	wash
microphone			

1 Read the words or phrases in the vocabulary box and then find the following:

1 Words that mean *quickly*.

2 Words that mean *turn on*.

3 The opposite of *sick*.

4 Two words that describe what you do to fruit or vegetables before you eat them.

5 Words that mean *to visit* or *to put in*.

2 With your partner, play a word game. Pick a word from the vocabulary box. Read the word. Tell your partner what it means.
- Use a stopwatch or set a timer for 30 seconds.
- How many times can you write the word in 30 seconds?
- How many times can your partner write the word in 30 seconds?
- Repeat with another word.

Remember ☆☆☆

A **prefix** is a group of letters at the beginning of a word. When we add a **prefix**, it changes the meaning of the word. For example: *un + helpful = unhelpful*.

Project 3 – How it works

> **Look and learn**
>
> We can build words by adding **prefixes**. Understanding a **prefix** can also help us to work out the meaning of a word.
>
> For example: cycle, bicycle (bi- means two, so a bicycle has two wheels).
>
> Here are some other examples of prefixes we can use when we describe machines:
>
> | Prefix | Meaning | Example word |
> |---|---|---|
> | micro- | very small | microwave |
> | aero- | in/of the air | aeroplane |
> | mono- | one | monoplane |
> | tri- | three | triangle |
> | e- | electronic | e-reader |
> | tele- | far, at a distance | telephone |
> | auto- | self, by itself | automatic (car) |

3 Copy the table below in your notebook. These words all have prefixes. Can you fill in the whole words and/or the missing meanings?

(Hint: You may know some of these prefixes from words in Maths and Science).

Prefix	Ending	Whole word	Meaning
uni-	cycle	unicycle	a cycle with _____ wheel
bi-	cycle	bicycle	a cycle with two wheels
bi-	ped	biped	an animal with _____ legs
centi-	metre	centimetre	100 in a metre
centi-	ped	centipede	an animal with _____ legs
tri-	angle	triangle	a shape with three sides
tri-	cycle	tricycle	a cycle with _____ wheels
kilo-	gram	kilogram	1000 grams
kilo-	metre	kilometre	_____ metres

4 Copy these words into your notebook and circle the prefixes.

automobile   television   microwave   tripod   bicycle   tricycle   telephone

Let's read

1. Look at the text below. What do you think the author is trying to do? Choose the best answer:
   - tell a story (entertain us)
   - make us want to buy something (persuade us to do something)
   - teach us how to use something (instruct us).

The Healthy Helper

This amazing new machine makes healthy drinks in a jiffy!

You can make your own fresh fruit and vegetable juice every day.

The machine is easy to use. It is also easy to clean.

You get an extra cup and a lid with the machine.

You can make your fresh juice in the morning. Then take it to school with you for a healthy drink at break time.

You'll wonder how you did without it!

2. Why did you choose the answer you did in Activity 1? Think about the types of verbs and adjectives used.

3. 1 Read the text again. In your notebook, make a list of the ways that the text makes The Healthy Helper seem like a good thing.

   2 Share your list with a partner and listen to theirs. Can you think of any negative things about *The Healthy Helper* that the text might not tell us?

4 Work in pairs to discuss the questions below.

   1 Find two adjectives that describe the machine in the first sentence of *The Healthy Helper*. Are they positive or negative words?

   2 Why do you think the author chose those words?

   3 Can you think of any other words to use instead? Do they make the machine sound better or worse?

5 Rewrite the advertisement using your own adjectives. Try to make it sound as terrible as possible, without changing any of its features. Here is an example of the first line:

   This rusty old machine makes stinky drinks in a jiffy!

6 Share your rewritten advertisement with the class. Whose advertisement will sell the least machines?

7 Find out how *The Healthy Helper* works and read the instructions. They are jumbled up. Copy the flow chart into your notebook and write the instructions in the correct order.

   • Leave for 30 seconds.
   • Wash or peel the fruit and veggies.
   • Add water or ice.
   • Put the cup and blade on the motor.
   • Switch on the machine.
   • Pop them in the cup.
   • Your healthy drink is ready.
   • Turn off the machine.

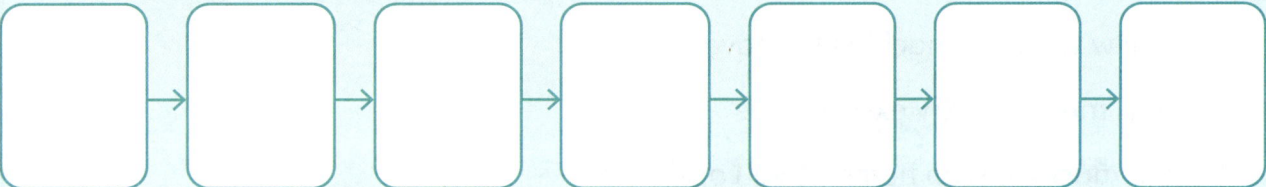

8 Discuss what would happen if you got the steps in the wrong order. Write a warning sentence to explain what might happen if you mix up two of the steps. For example: *If you turn off the machine before you pop the fruit and veggies in the cup, they will still be whole.*

9 Work in groups. Give the same instructions in Jamaican Creole (JC).

Term 1 Unit 1

Grammar builder

> **Look and learn**
>
> The **predicate of a sentence** always has a **verb**. The predicate can be one word or a group of words.
> For example:
> *The machine **helps**!*
> *This amazing new machine **makes healthy drinks in a jiffy**!*
> *You **get an extra cup and a lid with the machine**.*

1 Copy these sentences into your notebook. Circle the verb of each sentence and underline the complete predicate.

 1 The machine is easy to use.
 2 You can make your fresh juice in the morning.
 3 I take a healthy drink to school every day.
 4 The teacher has a new coffee machine.

2 Complete the predicates in the sentences.

 1 This machine is _____.
 2 I washed _____.
 3 Fruits and vegetables are _____.
 4 Switch _____.

3 Unscramble these words to make sentences that are grammatically correct and add punctuation.

 1 this machine wonderful drinks quickly makes
 2 a new washing machine we have
 3 that machine very expensive is
 4 the machine stop before it you open

4 In groups, search the newspaper or internet for a description of a new type of machine. Copy or print one paragraph, then exchange it with another group. Challenge that group to identify all the subjects and predicates in the paragraph in five or ten minutes.

Project 3 – How it works

Let's write

Background

Discuss machines you have seen or bought recently. Did they come with instructions? What sort of information did the instructions include?

Task

Work in pairs. You are going to make a flow chart to show a caveman or cavewoman how to use an everyday modern machine.

Plan

1. Choose a machine that you know how to use. Draw a picture of it or find a picture on the internet.

2. Write down your main ideas for instructions. Use the instructions for *The Healthy Helper* as a guide if you need to. Use eight sentences.

3. Read your instructions and improve them. Think carefully about the order that you tell your audience to do things. What details will be important, and what will be too complicated? Remember that the caveman or cavewoman has never seen your machine before!

4. Draw a flow chart like the one on the next page:

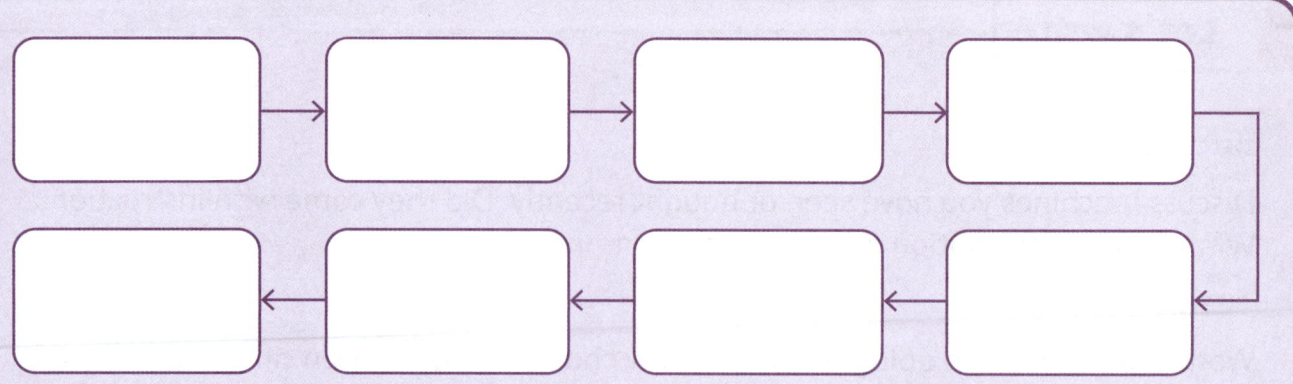

Write

5   Write eight instructions in the flow chart. Show the machine to the class. Then use your flow chart to explain how to use the machine.

Evaluate

6   As a class, think of one good thing about each presentation and one thing that could be improved. Use the "Editor's checklist" to help you.

Editor's checklist

When you finish your work, check it carefully.

- Have you used capital letters and full stops?
- Have you written eight sentences?
- Does each instruction have a verb?
- Are your instructions clear to someone who has never seen the machine before?
- Have you checked your spelling?
- Is the order of the instructions correct?

ICT opportunity

Search the internet for examples of instructions for machines. Can you find instructions for the items shown?

- What is the same about the instructions?
- What is different about the instructions?
- What makes the instructions easy to follow?

 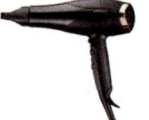

Project 4

Speaking and listening

1. Work with a partner to verbally give instructions on how to use a popcorn maker. Can you explain how to use the popcorn maker in five sentences? What verbs, technical vocabulary and nouns will you use?

Remember ☆☆☆

Be a good listener.
- Take turns speaking.
- Look at the person who is speaking.
- Think about what is being said.
- Ask the speaker questions.

2. Read through the instructions below. How do the instructions compare to yours? Is there anything missing or anything you would change?

   1. Put a cupful of popping corn (corn kernels) and 2 tablespoons of cooking oil into the machine.
   2. Put the lid on the machine.
   3. Plug the machine in and switch it on.
   4. Listen to the sounds. When the corn stops popping, switch the machine off.
   5. Put the popcorn into a bowl and season it with salt, spices or sugar.

3. Give instructions on how to use the popcorn maker to your partner as they role play making some popcorn. Swap over.

4. Which machines do you use at home? Role play how to make something using a simple machine. You can also film your demonstration and show the video to the class.

5 Work with a partner. Discuss and evaluate your demonstration.
- Did you speak clearly?
- Did you speak loud enough?
- Did you use technical vocabulary?
- Did you use expression and make your presentation interesting?

6 Pick a Jamaican Creole (JC) phrase about machines from a bag or box your teacher has prepared. Work in two teams to translate the phrase into Standard Jamaican English (SJE). Which team can translate the phrase first? Repeat.

Project 4 – Machines rule!

Word builder

Vocabulary box

machine	popping	to switch off	amazing
lid	season	automatic	instructions
to pop	spices	useful	vacuum cleaner
popcorn	to switch on	wonderful	

1. Read the words in the vocabulary box with your partner. Write down the words in one column. Now write the meanings next to the ones you know. Compare your lists and see if your partner knows any words you don't. Can you work out the meanings of any other words together? Check them in a dictionary and see if you are right.

Remember ☆☆☆

A **suffix** is a group of letters at the end of a word. When we add a suffix, we change the word. For example: *use + ful = useful*.

2. Copy the table into your notebook. Research suffixes and their meanings and complete the table by writing the meaning and an example word for each suffix.

Suffix	Meaning	Example word
-ful	full of	*use + ful = useful*
-er	describes what a machine or person does	*farm + er = farmer*
-less	without	*use + less = useless*
-ness		
-ly		
-ing		

41

3 Add *-ful* to these words and then write sentences with the adjectives you have made.

　　1　hope

　　2　wonder

　　3　pain

　　4　cheer

　　5　help

　　6　care

4 Add *-er* to the words below. If the word ends in *-e*, just add *-r*. Then work in groups and act the words out, while the group tries to guess the word.

　　1　play

　　2　ride

　　3　work

　　4　farm

　　5　write

　　6　make

I can work out the meaning of some words because I look for parts of words that I understand.

5 These words end in *-er* or *-or*. This usually means that they are nouns that name things or people that have a special job or function. Can you work out what they are and what they do?

　　1　a printer

　　2　a processor

　　3　a computer

　　4　a monitor

Project 4 – Machines rule!

Let's read

1. Work in pairs. Before you read this comic strip, look at the pictures. Tell your partner what you think the story is about.

2. Read the comic story.

The new vacuum cleaner

This is our new vacuum cleaner. It cleans the house by itself. It's very useful.

Aah! That's amazing!

Whirrrr

Dad switched on the machine.

Wow! This is wonderful. I can call my friends while it cleans the house!

Clickety-clickety-click

Cool! I can go and play while it cleans the house. Cheers!

Mmmmmm

Pick up your clothes, Kevin!

Eww!

You need to do your homework, Terri-Anne.

Wha-a-t?

3 Answer these questions about the story.

1 What did Dad buy?

2 What could the machine do?

3 Why did Mother throw the machine in the bin?

4 Look at the speech bubbles when Kevin, Terri-Anne and Mother see hear the vaccum cleaner. What emotion are they feeling? Explain how you know.

4 Work in groups and discuss the comic story.

1 Did you enjoy the story? Why?

2 Why do writers write comic stories?

3 Why do you think the pictures in a comic story are important?

4 Why are the speech bubbles useful in comics? Why wouldn't it be the same to write the words at the bottom of each picture? Would it be worse or better?

5 What do you call words such as *whirr* and *clank*? Can you find other examples in the story?

6 Draw two more comic frames to show what happens next. Make sure you include speech bubbles.

> **Remember** ☆☆☆
>
> Words that imitate the sound they are describing are **onomatopoeic**.

Grammar builder

Look and learn

Interjections are words or short phrases that express emotions. We can also use interjections to give more of an impact to what we are saying and make the words sound stronger.

We often put an exclamation mark (!) after an interjection. Remember that an interjection is not always a shout.

For example:

Interjection	When we use it
Ah!	When we suddenly understand something.
Phew!	When something is finished and we feel pleased that it is finished (or tired).
Oops!	When we make a mistake.
Oh, dear!	When we feel sorry or sad about something.

1 Read the comic strip again. Write down six interjections from the story.

2 Work in pairs. Look at the interjections in the comic strip and discuss why the author used each interjection. For example, *Wow!* shows that the character is impressed/amazed.

3 Look at the pictures and write down an interjection that each character could use.

4 Draw a cartoon picture like the pictures above. Include one or two people in the picture, each with a speech bubble. Put interjections in the speech bubbles.

Let's write

1. Reread the comic strip *The new vacuum cleaner* in the "Let's read" lesson. As a class, discuss and identify the onomatopoeic words used in the comic. Make a list of the onomatopoeic words in your notebook.

2. Work in pairs to create lists of onomatopoeic words for each machine below.

ICT opportunity

Research onomatopoeic words in an online dictionary or thesaurus. Create a podcast using onomatopoeic words to describe a machine of your choice.

3. Work in groups. Brainstorm some story ideas about a machine that gets out of control. Here are some questions to help you:
   - What sort of machine is it? What does it do?
   - How does it go out of control? Is there a cause?
   - What are the effects when it goes out of control?
   - Is the machine stopped? How?

4. Write your own story about a machine that gets out of control. Follow the steps given in the next page:

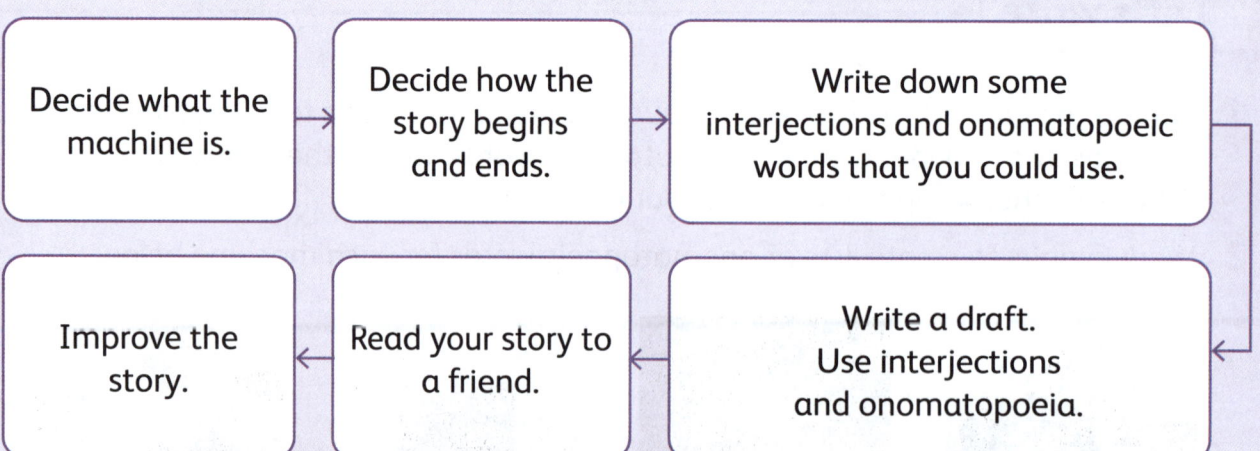

Remember

Punctuation is important. It helps the reader to understand the story. Make sure you are clear about when a character is excited or asking a question.

Editor's checklist

When you finish your work, check it carefully.

- Have you punctuated the story so that it can be understood by others?
- Have you used exclamations?
- Do all your sentences have subjects and predicates?
- Have you used question marks when needed?
- Is your story told in the past tense?
- Does your story have a beginning and an ending?

Evaluate

5 Now swap work with your partner and check his or her work against the "Editor's checklist".

- Underline the onomatopoeic words and draw a circle around the transitional words.
- Take turns to explain what you liked about each other's writing. If you think your partner has missed something from the checklist, explain how you would correct it. Make sure your comments are positive and clear.

6 Write two things you did well in your writing and give an example for each. Then write down what you would like to improve in your next piece of writing and how you will achieve this.

Project 5

Speaking and listening

1. Work in groups. Look at this photograph of one of the first computers. Describe the machine.

2. Can you imagine that computer being used today? Why/Why not?

3. As a class, list some of the places computers are used today. In groups, choose one place such as a school, supermarket or airport, and say how computers are used and how they make life easier. Select one person from the group to tell the class what you have discussed. You can copy the diagram below to help you organise your thoughts.

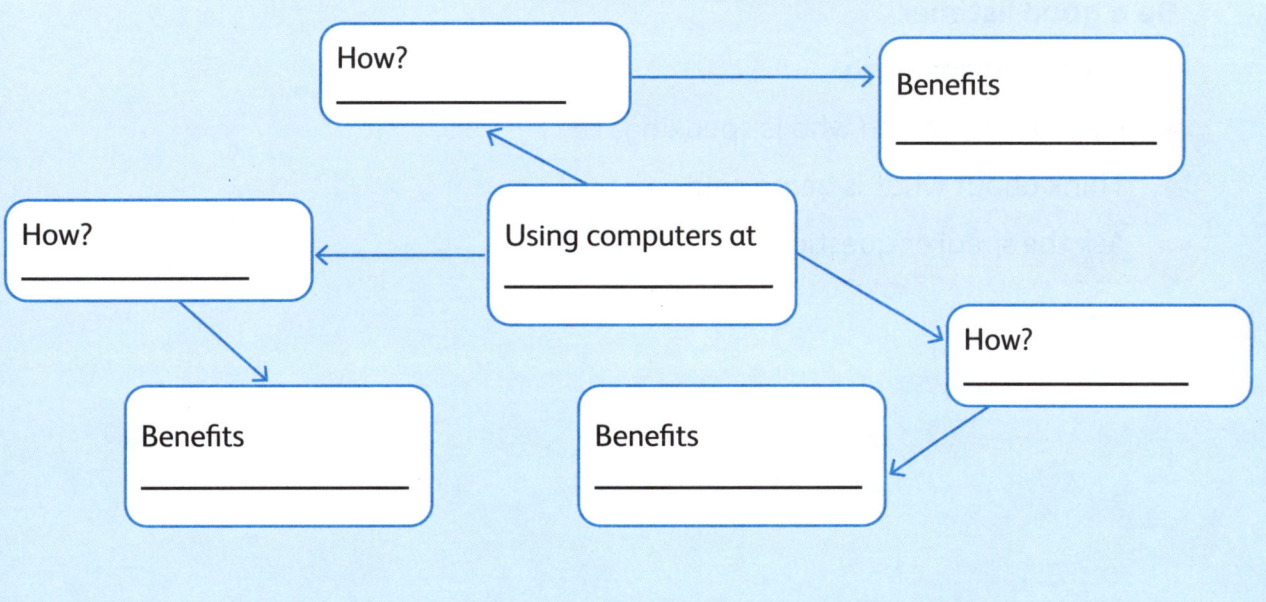

4 Do you think computers always make life easier for us? Why/Why not?

5 Work with a partner. Write common Jamaican Creole (JC) phrases about computers and translate them to Standard Jamaican English (SJE). Think about and include the different uses of computers.

Remember ☆☆☆

Be a good listener.
- Take turns speaking.
- Look at the person who is speaking.
- Think about what is being said.
- Ask the speaker questions.

Word builder

Vocabulary box

applications (apps)	disc drive	personal computer (PC)
battery	enough	printer
brand	keyboard	process
data	kit form	smartphone
demand	monitor	tablet
desktop	netbook	

1 Read the words in the vocabulary box. Make a list of all the words that are names of parts of a computer.

2 The following words from the vocabulary box are compound words. Write a sentence to explain what each word means.

   1 desktop

   2 personal computer

   3 keyboard

   4 smartphone

3 Work in pairs to spell the words below.

1	2	3
printer battery monitor smartphone computer data tablet		

- Copy this table on two sheets of paper, one for each student.
- Write the spelling words in the first column.

- Practise writing each word in the second column.
- Cover the first two columns and listen as your partner reads the words aloud.
- Write them in the third column.
- Then swap.

4 Looking at the structure of a word can help us to identify the meaning, read and spell words.

- Circle the prefixes.
- Underline the suffixes.
- Draw a line to split the compound words.
- Complete the grid by ticking or crossing the features. The first one is done for you.
- Add three words of your own.

Word	Prefix	Suffix	Compound word
unhelpful	✓	✓	
smartphone			
microwave			
microphone			
bicycle			
printer			
handlebar			
movement			
thunderous			
imagination			

5 In pairs, discuss how the structure of the word helps you to interpret the meaning. Pick one word and explain again to the class.

Project 5 – The first computers

Let's read

Did we really start there?

The first computers were huge, complicated and expensive machines that were operated by teams of people. Engineers, scientists and government officials used these first computers to process data. The computers were not suitable for home use.

Then, in the 1970s, small, cheap computers became available. They were sold in kit form. Each kit had a monitor or computer display, a keyboard, disc drives and a printer. You had to build the computer yourself!

Soon everyone wanted their own personal computer or *PC*, as it is usually called. You could buy a small and easy-to-use computer in the shops. So many people wanted these PCs that they often had to wait a long time for new stock to arrive in the shops. Brand names such as Commodore, Apple and TRS-80 became famous.

Where we started: Commodore PET, Apple, TRS-80

As the demand increased, the computers improved. People started to use computers to do their work, to play games and to communicate with other people. Today we can use small laptops or smart phones with applications (apps) that help us to do a wide range of things. We can take our computers with us wherever we go!

Where we are today: desktop computer, laptop, netbook, hybrid, tablet, smartphone

1 Read the text. What is the purpose of this text?

- to entertain
- to inform
- to persuade.

How do you know? What clues are there in the text to show the purpose? Can you identify any features of the text type?

2 Work in pairs. Answer the questions below.

1. Why did most people not have computers at home in the early days?
2. What did a computer kit consist of?
3. Name two computer brands that became famous.
4. Name two differences between the early computers and the computers we use today.

3 Look at each paragraph on the previous page. What is the main idea in each paragraph? Look for key words. Then write a subheading for the paragraph. The first one is done for you. Compare your subheadings with others in the class.

The first computers

The first computers were huge, complicated and expensive machines that were operated by teams of people. Engineers, scientists and government officials used these first computers to process data. The computers were not suitable for home use.

Research and study skills

Consider the different types of texts you have read so far during this unit on machines. Copy the table into your notebook and fill it in to identify the purpose and features of each text type.

Text type	Text	Purpose	Features
advertisement	Healthy Helper (p. 34)	to persuade	positive adjectives
poem	Song of the train (p. 20)	description	
story	The Machine (p. 24)		
instructions	Popcorn maker/ Healthy Helper (p. 34)		
information	Did we really start there? (p. 53)		
comic	The new vacuum cleaner (p. 43)		

Project 5 – The first computers

4 As a class, pick a machine. Write a list of questions that you would like to be able to answer about your machine. For example: When was it invented? How does it work? What is the most popular model/make?

ICT opportunity

Work in groups. Use the internet to research your chosen machine. Can you find the answers to your questions?

Consider:
- What text types will be most useful to share information about your machine?
- What features will help you find the information quickly? For example: *key words*, *subheadings*.

Make notes as you read. Record your answers.

5 Work in groups to create a poster about your chosen machine. Each group should choose a different purpose for the poster:
- to persuade the audience to buy the machine
- to entertain the audience (a story or poem about the machine)
- to inform the audience about the machine
- to instruct the audience (how to use the machine).

Use pictures, words and phrases. Ensure the purpose of your poster is clear.

6 Talk about the posters as a class. Do they look different? Why? Is the information on the posters different? Is there anything that is the same about the posters?

Grammar builder

> **L👀k and learn**
>
> The **subject of a sentence** is what or whom the sentence is about.
> The subject can be a noun, a pronoun or a name.
> The subject can be one word:
> **He** has a new laptop.
> **Amira** has good computer skills.
> The subject can be a group of words:
> **The first computers** were huge, complicated and expensive machines.
> **Engineers, scientists and government officials** used these first computers to process data.

1 Copy these sentences into your notebook. Underline the subject of each sentence.

   1 People wanted these new PCs.

   2 Each kit had a monitor or computer display, keyboard, disc drives and a printer.

   3 Kerri and Tyrone are doing some research on the laptop.

2 Add an adjective to each subject to make it longer. Underline the whole subject. For example: *The laptop is on the table. The <u>silver laptop</u> is on the table.*

   1 The boy is looking at the monitor of the computer.

   2 This computer is the best one you can buy.

   3 The computers were expensive and difficult to use.

3 Add a noun to each subject to make it longer. Underline the whole subject. For example: *Engineers used the first computers. <u>Engineers and scientists</u> used the first computers.*

1 Laptops are modern computers.

2 Sheldon is doing some research for his project.

3 You are practising the spelling words.

4 Unscramble these words to make sentences that are grammatically correct. Then add punctuation and underline the subjects.

1 wherever I go my laptop I take with me

2 computers the early expensive and big were

3 laptops small and smartphones many things can do

Term 1 Unit 1

Let's write

Task

You are going to write an information text about a machine. Choose a machine to write about.

ICT opportunity

Research your chosen machine and make notes in your notebook. You could also find some pictures of your chosen machine.
- What does it look like?
- How does it work?
- Can you name the main components?
- What can it do?
- Why is it useful?

Plan

1. Use a mind map to organise your ideas and plan what you are going to write about.

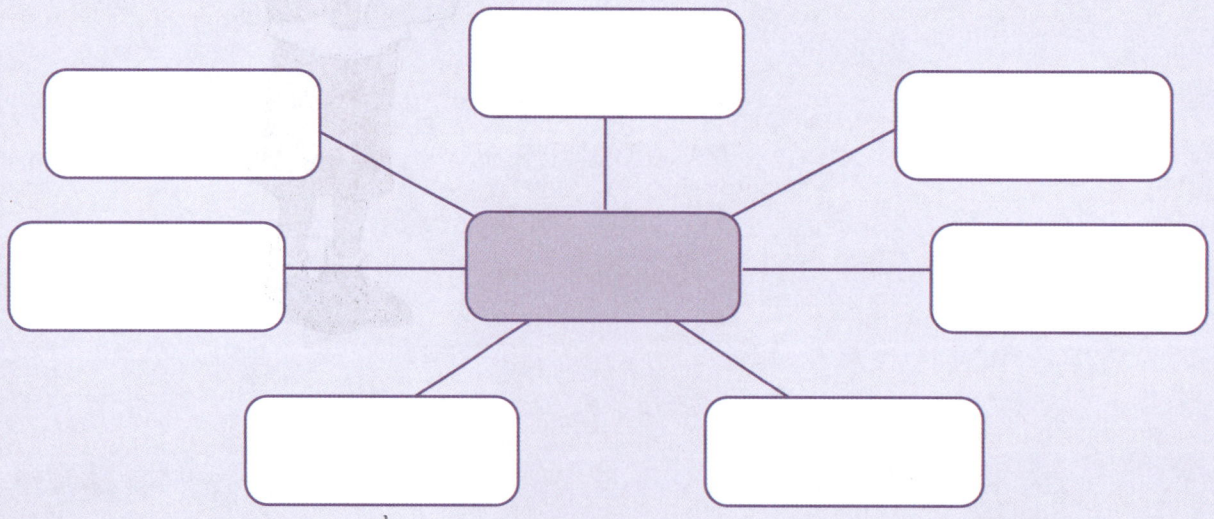

58

2. Consider the following points before you start writing and add to your plan:
   - a title
   - subheadings
   - a labelled diagram
   - three paragraphs
   - transitional words.

3. Draft your paragraphs. Start with your topic sentence and write another three sentences for each paragraph. Try to write long and short sentences.

Remember

The **topic sentence** gives the main idea of the paragraph. Make sure your sentence has at least one verb.

Write

4. Write your information text about your chosen machine.

Editor's checklist

When you finish your work, check it carefully.
- Did you describe the machine?
- Did you describe the machine and how it works?
- Did you use the correct vocabulary?
- Did you include a diagram with labels?
- Did you use headings?
- Did you use topic sentences?
- Did you say why the machine is useful?
- Did you check your spelling?

Evaluate

5. Now swap work with your partner and check his or her work against the "Editor's checklist". Take turns to explain what you liked about each other's writing. If you think your partner has missed something from the checklist, explain how you would correct it. Make sure your comments are positive and clear.

6. Write two things you did well in your writing and give an example for each. Then write down what you would like to improve in your next piece of writing and how you will achieve this.

Project 6

Speaking and listening

1. Work in pairs. Look at this picture of an imaginary machine. Describe the machine to your partner. Say what the machine looks like and what you think it does.

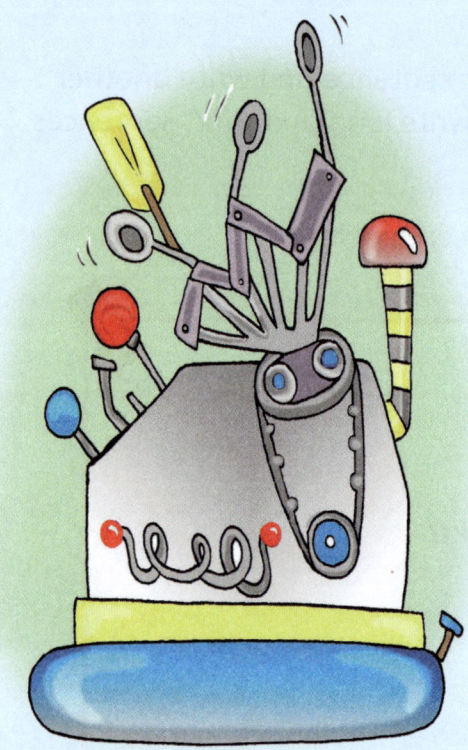

2. Work alone. Draw a picture of an imaginary machine that you would like to make. Think of a name for your machine.
   - Don't make it too complicated.
   - Don't show the drawing to anyone.

3. Work in pairs again, sitting back to back. You each need your drawings of imaginary machines, a pencil and a blank sheet of paper. You are going to give your partner instructions to draw the picture you have already drawn. Your partner needs to listen very carefully to your instructions and draw the picture. Compare the pictures when your partner has finished drawing.

Project 6 – Imaginary machines!

4   Discuss how to describe your drawings differently next time to make it even clearer for the person drawing to understand you.

5   Finally, come together and make a class performance of the poem. Try to find a real audience to appreciate your work!

ICT opportunity

- Work in groups. Invent a machine to be used in one of the following places:
    - in an office
    - to build a road
    - on a farm
    - on a boat.
- Give your machine a name that helps to describe what it does. If you can, make the name a compound word.
- Make a presentation about your machine to share with the class. Make sure you answer these questions:
    - What is the machine's name?
    - What does it look like?
    - What does it do?
    - Who would use it?

Word builder

Vocabulary box

| imaginary | classwork | contraption | snap | plus |
| real | homework | perfect | drop | switch |

1. Find two compound words in the vocabulary box. Write the words and circle the two words from which each compound word is made. Write a sentence to explain what each compound word means. Check your meanings in the dictionary. Were you right? If not, write a new sentence to explain the word.

2. Sometimes we can guess what a word means if we read a sentence with the word. Can you guess what the underlined words in these sentences mean? Choose the best answers.

   1. What is that funny <u>contraption</u>? It looks like a robot but it isn't a robot.
      - a big boat
      - a strange machine
      - a computer

   2. To start the engine, just <u>snap</u> on the switch.
      - turn
      - clap
      - break

L👓k and learn

If you look in a dictionary, you will see that there are many words that have part of the word *imaginary* in them. They are all part of the same **word family**:

image (a noun), **imag**ine (a verb), **imag**ery (a noun), **imag**ination (a noun)

We can change words into nouns by adding suffixes such as *-ation*.

3 Fill in the gaps in this table about words from the word family of *real*. Check your table with your partner. Have you filled in the same meanings and sentences? Which ones are correct? Use a dictionary to check.

Word	Noun, verb or adjective?	Meaning	Sentence
real	adjective	actual	I woke up and found out it wasn't a real contraption.
	verb	understand or find out	I didn't _____ I would need to use a laptop at school today.
realistic	adjective		
reality			It was nice to get back to reality after that nightmare.
realisation	noun		

Syllables

A **syllable** is a unit of sound. You can clap a word to work out how many syllables it has.

bike   toast/er   com/put/er

4 How many syllables do each of these words have? Clap each word. Write the words in your notebook and draw lines to show the syllables in each word.

kettle   laptop   hairdryer

printer   microwave   television

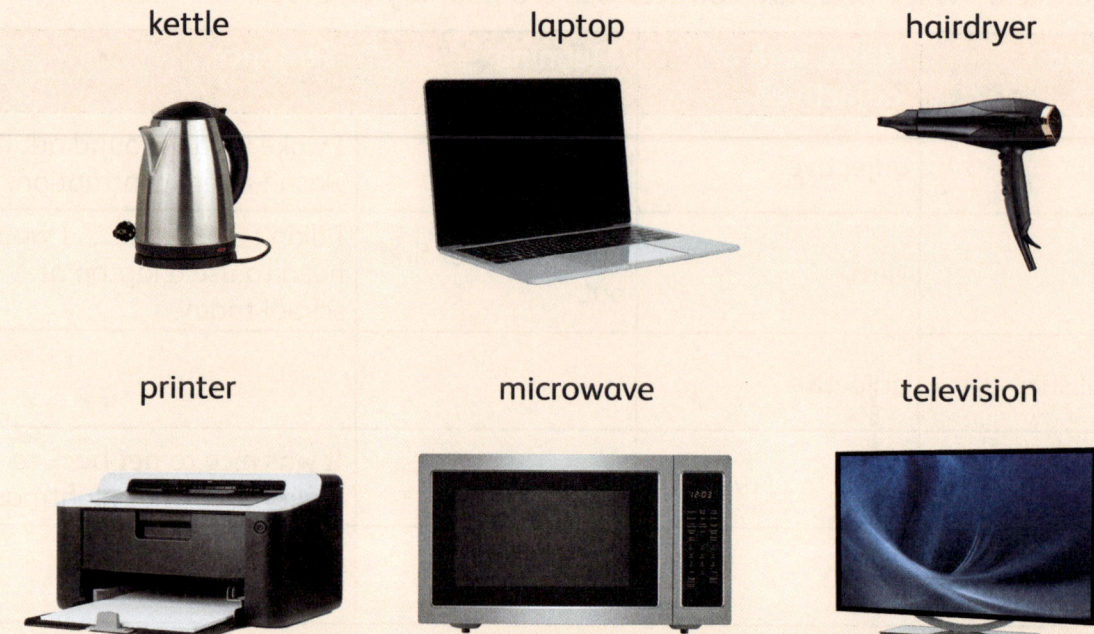

5 In a group, discuss all the different strategies you can use to identify unknown words and work out the meaning or pronunciation. How can each of the following help?

- sight recognition
- syllables
- prefixes
- suffixes
- compound words
- context
- word families
- using a dictionary

Discuss which strategies you find most useful and why.

Project 6 – Imaginary machines!

Let's read

1. Look at the poem below.
   - What is the name of the poem?
   - Who wrote the poem?
   - Is the poem about a real or an imaginary machine?
2. Read the poem aloud.

> **The headpiece**
> I have a special headpiece
> - the perfect machine
> Allows me to be alone … on my own
> Gives me peace
> And quiet …
> Pop on my headpiece
> - my afternoon routine
> Walk under the trees …
> Close my eyes and breathe
> Peace and quiet …
> "Ouch!" What was that?
> "Look where you walk!" someone squawks.
> Open eyes
> Apologise
> No longer alone or on my own
> No more peace and quiet.

3. Discuss these questions about the poem.
   - What does this machine do?
   - Does the machine work well?
4. What do you think the poet was trying to do when they wrote this poem? Why?
   - to make us laugh
   - to make us think
   - to make us angry
5. Would you like a machine like this? Why/Why not?
6. How is the machine in the poem similar or different to a machine that you know?

7 This is a rhyming poem. Can you find the words that rhyme? Say the words aloud. Then write them down. Look at how the words are spelled. Can you see any spelling patterns? Do you know of other words that are spelled like this?

Remember ☆☆☆

Words that **rhyme** have the same end sounds. The spelling may be different.

For example: *three, sea, bee*

8 Learn the poem *The Headpiece*. Recite the poem to the rest of your class, using actions – now you are showing them the machine! Think hard about how to say the lines. Try to make it clear how you are feeling as you say each line, for example, *happy, sad, excited, peaceful*.

9 Draw a comic strip showing what happens in the poem. Use some of the words of the poem in speech bubbles.

Research and study skills

1 Identify your strengths as a reader and one thing to improve on. Try to give an example.

- Can you recognise lots of words by looking at them?
- Can you decode words you don't know?
- Can you read fluently?
- Can you read with expression?
- Can you identify features and organisation of different text types?
- Can you understand what texts are saying and find information to answer questions?

2 Copy and complete the sentences in your notebook.

When reading I can _____. For example, _____ .

I would like to get better at _____. When I am reading I can do this by _____ .

Grammar builder

1. Copy these sentences into your notebook. Circle the subjects and underline the predicates.

   1. A homework machine is a wonderful idea.
   2. Kelly and Jo make their fresh juice every morning.
   3. That silly poem really made me laugh!
   4. The first personal computers were huge and very expensive.

2. Add subjects to these sentences.

   1. _____ drew an interesting imaginary machine.
   2. _____ loved the poem about the headpiece.

3. Complete the predicates in these sentences.

   1. That little machine can make _____.
   2. A bicycle has _____.

4. Correct the grammatical mistakes in the paragraph by changing the underlined words to the past tense.

   Last week we <u>buying</u> a popcorn machine. We <u>are</u> so excited. We <u>takes</u> it from the box and <u>follows</u> the instructions. Soon we <u>have</u> a lovely fresh bowl of popcorn! Father <u>says</u>, "What a wonderful machine!"

5. Add interjections to this direct speech to make it more interesting. Then practise saying them to show anger, fright or happiness.

   1. It's a very big machine.
   2. I am so tired.
   3. Now I understand what you mean.
   4. I made a mistake.

Remember

Sentences have two parts: a **subject** and a **predicate**. The subject and the predicate can be one word or a group of words.

Let's write

1. Discuss in small groups ideas for an imaginary machine.
   - What will the machine look like?
   - What will the machine do?
   - What will it sound like?
   - How will the machine work?
2. Draw a detailed diagram of your imaginary machine. Add labels to your picture.
3. Make a list of onomatopoeic words to describe the sound of your imaginary machine working.
4. Plan a poem about your imaginary machine. Jot down ideas, words and phrases for your poem.

> **Remember** ☆☆☆
>
> Remember what you have learned about **rhythm** and **rhyme** in the poems you have read. Decide whether you want your poem to be happy, sad, funny or exciting.

Evaluate

5. When you are happy with your poem, write it out neatly and display it in the classroom for others to read. Read your poem out loud. Do you like how it sounds?
6. Write in your notebook two things you did well in your writing and give an example for each. Then write down what you would like to improve in your next piece of writing and how you will achieve this.

Term 1 Unit 1 Review and assessment

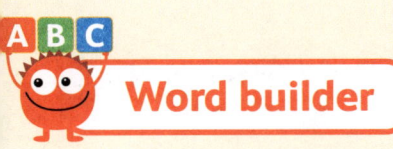

Word builder

1   Make as many compound words as you can by combining the following words.

   ship   night   fall   length   man   wave
   water   light   micro   yard   wreck   stick

2   Write a sentence for each onomatopoeic word. For example: *The microwave finished with a ping!*

   ping   pop   beep   bang

3   Form adjectives from the words in brackets. Then use them to complete the sentences.

   1   Our teacher says Marilyn is very _____ as she recycles plastic bottles as planters. (resource)

   2   Some of the most _____ sunsets can be seen from Negril Point. (beauty)

   3   It was a _____ moment when we heard the screech of tyres and then the loud bang. (dread)

   4   Thank you, it was _____ of you to look after the book I left behind yesterday. (thought)

   5   Paige is such a _____ dancer! (grace)

Let's read

1 Read the instructions and answer the questions.

How to use the CleanAll vacuum cleaner

The new CleanAll vacuum cleaner is easy to use. Insert a clean bag and then attach the extension wand to the machine. Select the attachment that you need and put it on the extension wand. Pull out the retractable electrical cord by pressing on the blue button. Then plug the cord into a wall socket. Switch on the machine and you are ready to start cleaning!

When you have finished, switch off the machine and unplug it. Pull the cord gently and it will go back inside the machine. Store your machine away carefully.

Warnings:

- Do not let the plug or the electrical cord get wet.
- Do not hold the end of the attachment on your clothes.

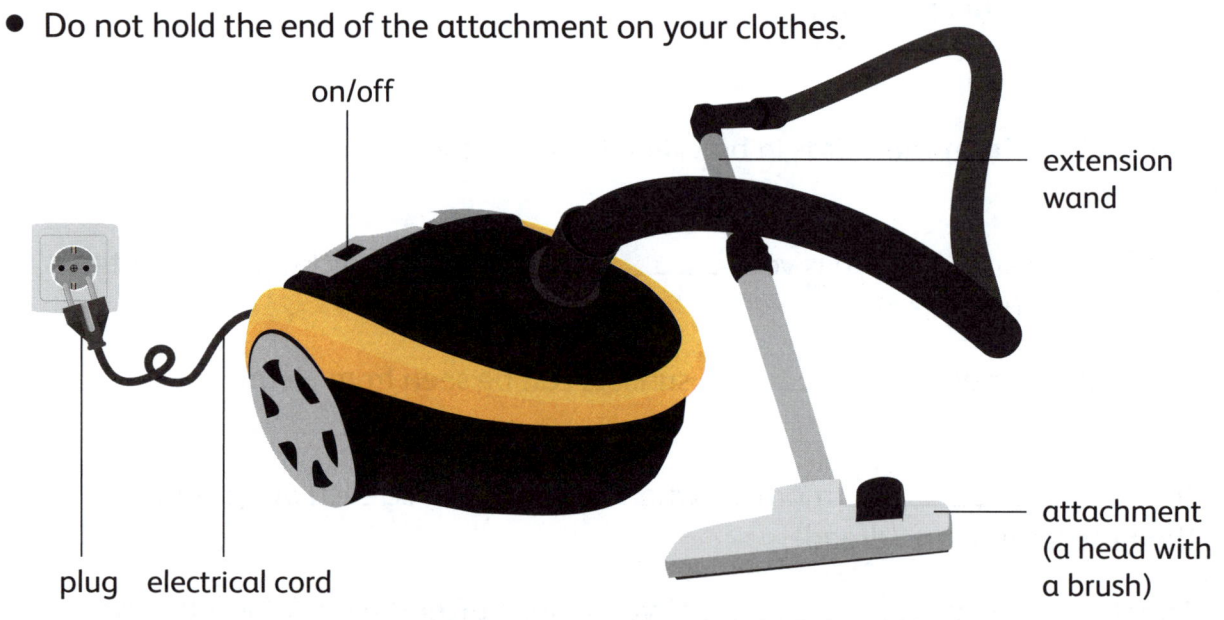

1. What kind of machine is a CleanAll?
2. Write down three things that you have to do before you start this machine.
3. Find a word in the text that describes the electrical cord and that tells us that the cord goes back into the machine when you are not using it.
4. Do you use a vacuum cleaner at home? What do you do with it? Write two sentences.
5. Is it a good idea to try and vacuum your clothes? Why?
6. Mime how to use the vacuum cleaner. Use gestures to show what you should and should not do.

Review and assessment

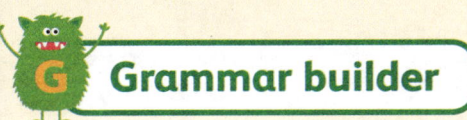

Grammar builder

1. Venessa made the following journal entry, but there are subject–verb agreement errors. Rewrite the journal entry, correcting the errors.

> I must start taking better care of myself so that I can stay healthy. Nurse Campbell visited our class today to talk about our health and well-being. I now knows that several things work together to keep us healthy. If we does not eat healthy foods we puts ourselves at risk.
>
> Diabetes are likely for persons who consume too much sugary and processed foods. Heart attacks is also a possible effect of poor food choices, especially foods loaded with bad fats that clogs the arteries.
>
> Lack of exercise also have an effect on our health and well-being. Lack of exercise lead to weight issues that puts pressure on our organs. When our organs is overworked, they malfunctions and causes health complications. To avoid this we must get at least 35 minutes of physical activity every day. So even though we likes to surf the web and play computer games we needs to go outside and play or we are putting ourselves at risk.
>
> Did you know that mental health can also affect your well-being? Stress affect the way our bodies function. Sometimes persons gets so stressed that it affect their sleep. Over time, the lack of sleep slow their brain activity and the fatigue from their bodies cause them to move slowly and make mistakes. This can be very dangerous. I definitely need to take better care of myself as I do not want to be unhealthy!

Let's write

- Here is a selection of titles:
  - The revenge of the computer
  - How to use this machine
  - The best machine in the world
  - A most marvellous machine
- Choose one title. Write a text to go with the title. Your text can be one of the following:
  - a poem
  - a description
  - a story.
- In your writing, demonstrate that you:
  - can write complete sentences with the correct punctuation
  - can write grammatically correct sentences
  - can spell the words that you use correctly.

Don't forget to check and edit your work before you hand it in for assessment!

71

TERM 1

Unit 2

Project 7

Speaking and listening

1. Have a class discussion about the environment around you. Here are some questions to think about:
   - What can you see and hear?
   - What or who lives in your environment?
   - What do you need from the environment?
   - What does the environment need from you?

2. Go on a walk around your school yard or community with your teacher. What can you see and hear? Observe how people are interacting with the environment.
   - Are there any animals?
   - Are there any plants?
   - What are the people doing?

   Draw a table to complete during your walk. Draw and label or write about what you can see and hear on your table.

Place	What you can see	What you can hear

3. Tell your class what you saw and heard on your walk in a short presentation. Answer any questions your class might have.
4. Listen carefully to others present what they found and ask questions.

How to prepare a good presentation:
- Speak clearly and loud enough for everyone to hear.
- Use expression to make it sound interesting.
- Use an appropriate tone to suit the purpose. Is it an important point you are making or do you want to entertain and make people laugh?
- Sequence your main points in order.

Term 1 Unit 2

Word builder

Vocabulary box

balancing	breeze	swinging	thud
laughing	flew	still	toppled
branch	chirping	prancing	trunk
fell	coconut	swinging	shouting

1. As a class, read all the words in the vocabulary box aloud together. You may have used some of these to describe what you could see and hear in the school yard.

2. Write the following words in alphabetical order:

branch	swinging
flew	breeze
trunk	still
toppled	

> If two or more words begin with the same letters, look at the second and third letters of the words, just like you do when you look in the dictionary.

3. Find the following words in a dictionary. Write down the meaning of each word in your own words.

Word	Meaning
balance	
laugh	
topple	

4. With your partner, play the *Dictionary dash* game. Race against others in your class. Have your dictionary in front of you ready and listen to your teacher call out a word to find. Who can find each word in the dictionary first?

ICT opportunity

You could use an online dictionary to check the meaning of words.

Let's read

1. Trees are an important part of our environment. Talk about the following questions.
   - Why do people need trees?
   - Why do wild animals need trees?

2. Read this poem. Role play the poem in small groups to show that you understand it. Let one person read the poem while the others act.

Being a tree

One time
I stood on the arm of the sofa
balancing on one leg
my arms spread wide
like branches.

I was a gigantic tree
in the deep green forest.
Many birds sat on my branches
chirping their happy songs.
Small animals nestled by my trunk
prancing and playing, being free.
And just as a blue jay
was about to land on my branch
Mom shouted. "Be careful!"
The blue jay flew away.
I fell, and my tree toppled over.

by Opal Palmer Adisa

3. The poet describes what he or she did to act like a tree using similes and metaphors. Can you find the examples below in the poem?

   My arms spread wide _____.

   I was _____.

   I fell and _____.

Term 1 Unit 2

> ### L👀k and learn
>
> **Similes** and **metaphors** are figures of speech that many poets use to create word pictures for their readers. Similes and metaphors compare things to help us understand them better.
>
> **Simile**
>
> Similes are direct comparisons. You often find the words **like**, **as**, **such as** or **…-er than** in a simile.
>
> For example: *I spread my arms spread wide **like branches**.*
>
> *Listen to the wings, **lighter than eyelashes** …*
>
> *I can run **as fast as** a hare.*
>
> **Metaphor**
>
> Metaphors are indirect comparisons. We compare things, but we don't use the words **like** or **such as**.
>
> Sometimes we also give human qualities to objects or other living things.
>
> For example: *I **was a gigantic tree**. Many birds sat on **my** branches.*

4 Look at the examples below. Work with your partner and decide whether they are similes, metaphors or neither.

   1 The sea was as cold as ice yesterday.
   2 "This classroom is a zoo today!" said the teacher.
   3 My father is a night owl because he stays up late.
   4 The trees rustled in the breeze.
   5 I had to wait for my sister to finish football practice and it was like watching paint dry.
   6 The water shimmered in the moonlight.

5 Discuss with a partner. What is the author's purpose for this poem? How do you know?
   - to entertain
   - to inform
   - to make the reader laugh
   - to persuade
   - to instruct

6 Look at the poem again. What can you picture when you read it? How does it make you feel? Compare your ideas with a partner.

7 Find other poems or texts about trees or the environment to read. You could search the internet or look at the library. Do they all have the same purpose? Create a list for the class.

8 Choose another text about trees and compare it to the poem. In your notebook, draw and complete a table like the one below.

Similarities	Differences

What's your view?
Is it important to care for trees?
What can we do to look after them?

Grammar builder

Mark	When to use	Examples
capital letter	for names at the beginning of sentences	Dionne Brand The poem is about acting like a tree.
full stop (.) question mark (?) exclamation mark (!)	at the end of sentences	This is my hat. Do you know that poem? What a great song!
comma (,)	to separate words in a list	birds, insects and snakes live in trees.
semi-colon (;)	to show that two sentences are related	I planted flowers; my dad planted a tree.
speech marks or inverted commas ("")	to show that someone is speaking	"Be careful!" Mom shouted.

1 Rewrite these sentences. Use punctuation marks from the box above.

1. people wild animals insects and birds all share this environment
2. can you hear the wind whispering in the trees
3. what a silly poem
4. listen to the sound of the hurricane shouted tyrone
5. we planted more trees in the garden you can never have too many trees
6. mum shouted don't jump on the couch
7. birds need trees so do insects and small animals

Project 7 – My world

Let's write

1. Read this acrostic short poem about living together and sharing our environment.

    Share what you have.

    Help to protect plants and animals.

    Always respect your environment.

    Remember that we need plants and animals.

    Enjoy what you have!

2. Now write your own acrostic poem. You can work with a partner or in groups. Think of a word to start with, for example *TREES* or *FOREST*.

    Remember ☆☆☆

    Write all your ideas and words in a mind map first. Then choose the best words.

Could you include a simile or metaphor in your poem?

3. As a class, write a checklist for your acrostic poems. What do you need to include? How should they look?

79

4 Use the "Editor's checklist" to edit your poem.

Editor's checklist

Check your work carefully when you finish.
- Do the first letters of each line spell out a word?
- Have you chosen words that help to create an atmosphere?
- Have you checked your spelling?

5 Once you are happy with your poem, write it out in your best writing or type on a computer and decorate it.

These are the Blue Mountains of Jamaica. If we care for our environment, we can all live together happily.

Project 8 – Different places, different experiences

Project 8

Speaking and listening

1. As a class, discuss when you use Jamaican Creole (JC) phrases and when you use Standard Jamaican English (SJE). Think about:
   - different environments/places
   - different situations
   - different people you might talk to or communicate with.

   Then create a table together, including some example phrases.

When we might use JC	When we might use SJE

2. Work with a partner to create a list of common Jamaican Creole (JC) phrases used in school/the school yard or your community. Then translate the phrases into Standard Jamaican English (SJE).

JC phrases	SJE phrases

81

Word builder

1 In the table below, there are some animals from different habitats around the world, such as the rainforest, the desert and grasslands. As a class, read the names of the animals aloud. Discuss what habitat you think each animal comes from.

2 Look at these consonant clusters. Say them aloud.

3 Find and circle the consonant clusters in each animal name. Some names have more than one cluster.

Clusters are groups of consonants. They can be found at the beginning, middle or sometimes the end of words.

4 Write the animal names in a table like the one below. Some names may go in more than one column. In the last column, add more words that contain each consonant cluster.

Consonant cluster	Animal name	Other words
bl	blue morpho butterfly	
br		
ch		
fl		
fr		
gr		
ph		
fr		
sc		
sl		
th		

5 Use a dictionary to find other words with these letter clusters.

Identifying consonant clusters in words we know can help us to pronounce unknown words.

6 Practise spelling these words. Use the consonant clusters to help you.

Spelling	1st attempt	2nd attempt	3rd attempt
butterfly			
cheetah			
sloth			
frog			
scorpion			
flamingo			

ICT opportunity

Research animals from different habitats, such as rainforests, grasslands and the desert. Can you use consonant clusters to help you pronounce the names of the animals found in these habitats?

7 Can you find the animal names in the word puzzle?

B	U	T	T	E	R	F	L	Y
Y	C	W	S	A	P	R	D	J
J	H	C	L	Z	R	O	S	L
A	E	J	O	L	H	G	C	S
P	E	H	T	E	S	T	O	D
Q	T	Z	H	F	X	U	R	F
A	A	O	W	J	K	Y	P	B
N	H	R	B	Q	D	O	I	E
F	L	A	M	I	N	G	O	B
M	G	U	X	T	Y	K	N	W

butterfly
scorpion
flamingo
sloth
frog
cheetah

8 Use squared paper to make your own word puzzle. Pick five animal names with consonant clusters. Write the names with one letter in each square. Fill the remaining squares with other letters. Give your puzzle to a partner. Can they find the hidden words?

Project 8 – Different places, different experiences

Let's read

1. Read this diary entry written by someone who travelled to Antarctica. Have you ever written a diary? What do you think the purpose of a diary is?

Antarctica – January

After eleven days aboard the ship *Grigoriy Mikheev*, we reached Antarctica. Some snow petrels flew towards the ship to welcome us. As we continued we saw some great orcas swimming past the ship. Some of the orcas had calves.

We sailed through some heavy ice and were able to see this land of Big Ice. There were some chinstrap penguins on the icebergs and the occasional leopard seal came to greet us.

The sun did come out a few times that morning. We were mesmerised by the ice, grey skies, white clouds and wind-whipped waters. When the ice became more and more dense, we could hear small icebergs knocking against our ship.

2. With a partner, decide which animal from the diary is shown in each picture. Discuss clues from the text that helped you.

3. Read the diary entry from South America.

San Pedro de Atacama – February

When we arrived at San Pedro de Atacama, the landscape was very different from the Antarctic. All we saw was sand and more sand. We were fortunate because we saw three llamas along the road as we drove to our hotel. The roads are all sandy and all the buildings have been built in red clay.

The next morning we took a bus trip and stopped on the Calama-San Pedro road, which overlooks the salt plains. We saw lots of red clay formations, too. They were so beautiful! From where we were standing we could see some green areas. Our tour guide told us that a lot of trees have died because the water is very salty. They planted the trees to provide food for the llamas but the trees are too thorny. The thorns hurt the mouths of the llamas.

A llama

Then we drove to the "Valley of Death". The valley has high walls of red clay and sand dunes. The walk through the valley was very, very hot and there was hardly any shade. At one point the walls of the valley were covered in salt. It looked like someone had sprinkled icing sugar on the surface of the red clay. If you listen carefully, you can hear the walls creaking as they start cooling in the evening.

After that we visited the Moon Valley. There are few plants and animals in this area because it is so hot and dry.

Filmmakers make films about the moon in Moon Valley.

ICT opportunity

Use the internet to find a map and locate both locations.

4   Copy this flow chart in your notebook and complete it to show the places that the diary writer visited in South America.

Research and study skills

1   Work in pairs to compare Antarctica with San Pedro de Atacama. Copy and complete this table in your notebook. Find the information in the texts you have read.

	Weather and climate	What the author did	Animals that live there	Landscape
Antarctica				
San Pedro de Atacama				

2   Tell your partner or your class what you have learned about these two different places. Use the information in the table you have completed.

Grammar builder

L👀k and learn

When we write, we try to **connect ideas**. This makes our style of writing more interesting for the reader.

We can link ideas with conjunctions such as **and**, **but**, **because**, **as** and **so**.

For example:

They planted the trees to provide food for the llamas. The trees are too thorny.

They planted the trees to provide food for the llamas, **but** *the trees are too thorny.*

When we give a reason for something, we join sentences with **because**.

For example:

A lot of trees have died. The water is very salty.

A lot of trees have died **because** *the water is very salty.*

1 Join these sentences with *and* or *but*.

1. The valley was very, very hot. There was hardly any shade in the valley.
2. We saw some chinstrap penguins. We saw some leopard seals.
3. Antarctica is very cold. Chile can be very hot.
4. Llamas live in Chile. They do not live in Antarctica.

2 Join these sentences with *because*.

1. There are few animals in the desert. It is too hot.
2. The houses are made of clay. There is a lot of clay in the area.
3. We wore warm clothes and thick caps and scarves. It was very cold.
4. She wants to visit Antarctica. She wants to see icebergs.

Project 8 – Different places, different experiences

Let's write

1. Imagine that you went on a journey to one of the places in the photographs below or a place of your choice. Write three to four paragraphs about your trip.

The Dunn's River Falls in Jamaica

The Blue Mountains in Australia

Here are some notes to help you plan your writing.

- Paragraph 1: Say where you went and why you went there. What word will be useful to connect your clauses here?

- Paragraph 2: Describe what the place (the landscape) looks like. Think about what metaphors or similes might help the class picture it.

- Paragraph 3: Describe the plants and animals you saw. Are there any useful figures of speech or exciting adjectives you can use?

- Paragraph 4: Say what you liked best about the journey and why.

2. As a class, write a checklist for your diary entry. What will you need to include? Use your class checklist to edit and improve your writing.

3. Evaluate your writing. Write these sentences in your notebook:

   I am really pleased with my writing because _____. I would like to improve my writing by _____.

Project 9

Speaking and listening

1. Discuss each set of pictures.
   - Where is the picture taking place?
   - What is happening in each picture?
   - In which order did the events take place?
   - How is the person interacting with or impacting on the environment?

Project 9 – What is the impact on the environment?

2 Choose one set of pictures and prepare a presentation to explain to your class what you think is happening, the order the events are taking place. You could also discuss the impact on the environment or how the person is interacting with the environment.

3 Listen carefully to members of your class during their presentation. Can you ask a question?

> How to prepare a good presentation:
> • Speak clearly and loud enough for everyone to hear.
> • Use expression to make it sound interesting.
> • Use an appropriate tone to suit the purpose.
> Is it an important point you are making or do you want to entertain and make people laugh?
> • Sequence your main points in order.

ICT opportunity

Find pictures of people at the park. Discuss with a partner:
- Where is the picture set?
- What is happening?
- How are the people interacting with their environment?

Word builder

Vocabulary box

accommodation	flooding	indigenous	sensitive
breeze	habitat	mangrove	suitable
development	housing	nowhere	greedy
environmentally			

1. Break these words up into syllables. This will help you to learn to pronounce and spell the words.

Example:
/suit/ /a/ /ble/

Clap the word to help count the syllables!

indigenous	sensitive
habitat	mangrove
accomodation	development

2. Read the sentences. Then look at the underlined words and work out the meaning of the words from clues in the sentence. Discuss the meanings with a partner.

   1. Jamaican coneys or hutia are <u>indigenous</u> to Jamaica. They are not found anywhere else in the world. They live on rocky, forested mountain sides.

   2. The wind started off as a soft <u>breeze</u> and then it became a gale!

   3. They were very <u>greedy</u>. They ate all the food and didn't leave anything for us!

   4. We are looking for <u>accommodation</u> for six people in Kingston. It could be a house or an apartment.

3. A **root word** is the main part of a word; we can add **prefixes** and **suffixes** to make other words. Draw a table like this one. Add suffixes and prefixes to the root words to make new words.

Root word	Other words using the root word
develop	development, developing, developed, undeveloped, developer, redevelop
build	
help	
care	
use	

When you are reading an unknown word try:
- breaking the word into syllables to help you pronounce it
- reading the whole sentence for context clues to work out the meaning
- looking for root words to work out the meaning.

L👀k and learn

To work out what a word means, look for parts of the word that you already know. For example: *development*

The verb *develop* means to grow or change.

-ment is a suffix that we often use to make nouns.

So, *development* is an activity that is related to growing and changing.

Let's read

1. Look at the text below. Where would you expect to see a text like this?
   - Read the title, look at the illustrations and the introductory sentences.
   - Say what you think this text is about.
2. Read the text silently by yourself or with a partner.

Is this the beginning of the end?

A new development is again on the cards for Kingston. And once again, there is a threat to the environment.

Jamaica is the third largest island in the Caribbean. Kingston, as the capital of Jamaica, is the main attraction for people wanting a city life. As Kingston is a major seaport with many businesses, people come to Kingston to look for work. As a result, there is a growing need for accommodation.

There is very little suitable land left to build houses. Large numbers of houses are therefore being built on the slopes of the mountains. This in turn is starting to affect the supply of water to the town. The housing developments are gradually destroying the natural habitats of indigenous animals. The Jamaican coney, which lives on rocky mountain slopes, is an example. Some of the breeding grounds of the black throat warbler birds have also been destroyed.

A mangrove that has been cleared

Closer to the sea, mangroves have been cleared to create space for housing developments. Mangrove forests are environmentally sensitive areas. The habitats of the animals that once lived there have been destroyed. Indigenous plants are also disappearing and as a result, the areas are now prone to flooding. The coastal waters are also being polluted by the housing developments. In other words, housing developments are threatening plant and animal life on land and at sea.

Do all the plants and animals have to die before we think about taking care of the land and water in which they live? How can we build houses and preserve the environment? There must be a way!

A black throat warbler

What is the purpose of this text?

3   Read the text carefully again and find the main ideas in each paragraph. Look for a topic sentence in each paragraph. Write down the main ideas.

4   Work in pairs. Make lists of the positive and negative effects of housing developments. Use ideas from the text you read.

The effects of housing developments

Positive (benefits)	Negative (harm)

5   Has the author talked more about positive effects or negative effects of new housing developments?

- What do you think they are trying to make you think about housing development?
- Can you think of any other effects of housing development (positive or negative)? Add these to your list.
- Can you think of any reasons why the author might not have mentioned some of these?

Keep this list as you will use it later.

Grammar builder

Look and learn

Verbs describe an action or something you can do. We can use them in the past, present or future tense. The **past** means the action has already happened, the **present** means the action is happening now and the **future** means the action is going to happen.

Past	Present	Future
I **ate** a mango.	I **am eating** a mango.	I **will eat** a mango.
I **fell** off the swing.	I **am falling** from the swing.	I **might fall** off the swing.
I **waited** for the bus.	I **am waiting** for the bus.	I **will wait** for the bus.

1 Copy the table into your notebook and sort the following words in the three columns.

built	am damaging	am breaking	will harm
am building	will damage	polluted	harmed
will build	broke	am polluting	am harming
damaged	might break	will pollute	

Past	Present	Future

2 Draw a table like the one below and fill in the missing verbs.

Past	Present	Future
I made.	I am making.	
	I am swimming.	I will swim.
I ran.		I will run.
	I am walking.	

3 Choose the correct verb tense to complete the sentences.

1 The bird flew / fly away when the cat came.

2 My friend fell / fall over in the school yard.

3 I am going to walk / walking to the park.

Project 9 – What is the impact on the environment?

Let's write

Task

You are going to write a short essay in which you explain what you think about housing developments in Jamaica.

Plan

1 Look at the notes you made earlier about the positive and negative effects of housing developments. Add any other points you have thought of since. Look at all the texts in this unit for help. Look at news reports, too.

2 Organise your thoughts. What do you think? Are the benefits more important or is the environment more important? Write a beginning and an ending for your essay that express your feeling.

Write

3 Now draft your arguments. Write one paragraph for each argument or idea. Remember to write a topic sentence for each paragraph. Then write two more sentences in which you explain the argument or idea.

Evaluate

4 Read your draft essay. Does it make sense? Have you linked your ideas? Write one good thing and one thing that you could improve about your essay. Explain what difference your improvements make.

Remember ☆☆☆

The **topic sentence** is the main idea of the paragraph.

Editor's checklist

Check your work carefully when you finish.

- Did you use linking words or phrases to connect your ideas and sentences?
- Did you write a topic sentence for each paragraph?
- Did you make your opinion clear?
- Did you use facts about the positive and negative effects to back up your opinion?

Project 10

Speaking and listening

1. What do you know about how people harm the environment? Share your ideas with the class before you read or listen to this poem.

2. Listen as your teacher reads this poem.

> **Dreamer**
>
> I dreamt I was an ocean
> and no one polluted me.
>
> I dreamt I was a whale
> and no hunters chased after me.
>
> I dreamt I was the air
> and nothing blackened me.
>
> I dreamt I was a stream
> and nobody poisoned me.
>
> I dreamt I was an elephant
> and nobody stole my ivory.
>
> I dreamt I was a rain forest
> and no one cut down my trees.
>
> I dreamt I painted a smile
> on the face of the Earth
> for all to see.
>
> *by Brian Moses*

3. Talk about the poem as a class. Think about:
   - What does the poem refer to?
   - What do you think the poet is trying to say?
   - How does the poem make you feel? Why?
   - What do you think the purpose of the poem is?

4. Practise reading the poem aloud and prepare to present to your class. Prepare a few sentences to tell your class what the poem is about and how it makes you feel.

Project 10 – Our natural resources

5 Give a short presentation to the class:
- Read the poem aloud.
- Tell your class what the poem is about and how it made you feel.

How to make a good presentation:
- Speak clearly and loud enough for everyone to hear.
- Use expression to make it sound interesting.
- Use an appropriate tone to suit the purpose. Is it an important point you are making or do you want to entertain and make people laugh?
- Sequence your main points in order.

Word builder

Vocabulary box

blackened	index	resources
chapter	ivory	source
contents	module	stream
disaster	ocean	unit
elephant	poisoned	whale
glossary	pollution	

1. Read all the words in the vocabulary box aloud. Use a pencil to divide each word into syllables. This will help you to pronounce the words and to remember how to spell them, for example: *chap/ter*.

2.
   1. Write a sentence for each word in the vocabulary box. Use the poem *Dreamer* to help you with the meanings of words you do not understand.

   2. Compare your sentences with your partner. Were there any words you were unsure of? Look them up in a dictionary together.

3. Choose two words from the vocabulary box that could be used to describe the photograph below. Use them to write one or two sentences about what you can see.

4. Find these words in the vocabulary box:

   1. a synonym for *the sea*

   2. a word that means *a small river*

   3. two names of animals

   4. a word that means the opposite of *success*

   5. a word that has a silent *h* in it.

100

Project 10 – Our natural resources

Let's read

1. Have you read many non-fiction books? Do you know how to find out what they are about and find information in them quickly? Discuss the ways you might be able to find:
   - a chapter about something you are interested in
   - the page number of a specific fact
   - the meaning of a word you don't understand.

Research and study skills

Read the contents page below and answer the questions.

Contents

Module 1	What is water?	4
Module 2	Where does water come from?	6
Module 3	Rivers and lakes	8
Module 4	Wetlands	14
Module 5	The oceans	18
Module 6	Underground water	24
Module 7	The water cycle	26
Module 8	Some interesting facts	28
Glossary		29
Index		30

1. What is this book about? Is it a story book about water or is it a non-fiction book about the water resources on Earth?

2. On which pages could you read about the water cycle?

3. On which pages would you find information about the sea?

4. Which module would you read if you had a project on rivers?

5. You need information on "sources" of water. You are not sure what the word *source* means. Where would you look first?

101

> **L👀k and learn**
> The **contents page** is a list at the beginning of a book of its main headings. It shows the parts into which the book is divided, for example chapters, modules or units. The contents page also gives the number of the page on which the part starts. This helps us to find the information that we are looking for.

2   **1**   The author of this book has written headings for the information in each module. Do you think this was a sensible choice? Explain why.

      2   What other features could the author use to help the reader find information?

3   Here is part of a glossary. Read the glossary and answer the questions.

> **habitat:** place where a living thing prefers to live or grow
> **pollution:** occurs when the air, land or water becomes dirty and dangerous
> **source:** where something comes from or begins
> **sustainable:** using energy and natural resources in a way that does not use them all up or harm the environment

      1   What do we call a place where a wild animal lives?

      2   Would the source of a river be where the river begins or ends?

      3   Name two things that can cause pollution.

      4   Do you think wind is a sustainable source of energy? Why?

      5   Do you think that this part of a glossary is from the same book as the contents on the last page? Explain your ideas.

> **L👀k and learn**
> A **glossary** is an alphabetical list of words with their meanings.

Project 10 – Our natural resources

4 Read this extract from the index of a book and answer the questions.

Drought   34–35
    Map of drought-prone areas   32
    Prevention measures   35
Earthquakes   36–39
    Map of earthquake zones   32
    Measuring strength of   38
    Most powerful   39
Famine   16
Floods   40–43
    Map of flood-prone areas   32
    Prevention measures   43
Hurricanes   44–48
    Case studies   46
    Diagram of   45
    Preparing for   47
    Warning systems   48

1. What do you think this book is about? What clues have you used to guess? On what pages would you find information about:
   - preparing for a hurricane
   - the world's strongest earthquakes
   - where in the world you are likely to experience a drought
   - how you could prevent flooding?

2. Discuss how the index is different from the contents you have already looked at. In your group, think of three times you would need to use the contents of a book, and three times you would use the index.

Look and learn

The **index** is an alphabetical list of all the main topics in a non-fiction book. It also gives the page number(s) to show you where you can find information about the topic. It is usually at the back of the book.

Grammar builder

Look and learn

A **verb** describes an action or something you can do.

An **adverb** tells us how the action was done. Adverbs often end in *-ly*.

Verbs	Adverbs
swam	slowly
ran	quickly
walked	carefully
jumped	happily
danced	mindfully

1. Underline the adverbs in these sentences.

   1. The children regularly recycled wastepaper.
   2. Elephants are sadly hunted for their ivory.
   3. The whale swam away from the boat quickly.
   4. The water slowly trickled over the rocks.

2. Choose an adverb to complete each sentence.

   carefully   carelessly   dangerously   unfortunately   helpfully

   1. The volunteers _____ cleaned the stream.
   2. _____, too many rainforest trees are being cut down.
   3. The children _____ sorted the litter for recycling.
   4. Plastic bottles _____ pollute the oceans.
   5. Rubbish was thrown away _____.

3. Work with a partner to create a list of adverbs you could use in your writing.

Project 10 – Our natural resources

Let's write

Task

Work in groups. Your task is to draw up a contents list for a 16-page booklet entitled *Animals that live in the sea*. Follow the instructions below.

Plan

1. Discuss what information you will put in your booklet. Brainstorm your ideas and write them on a mind map.

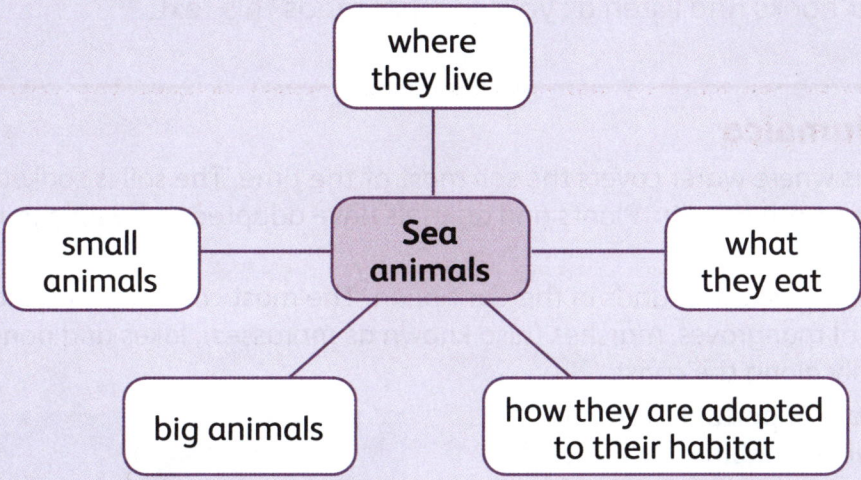

2. Decide how many sections your booklet will have. Think about the number of pages you have. Think of an appropriate name for each section. Make sure it summarises what is in the section to make information easy to find.

Write

3. Write your contents page out neatly. Remember that the reader will not have read the book yet.

Extra challenge

Draw up a glossary of ten words for your booklet on animals that live in the sea. Here are some words that you could include in the glossary. You can include your own words, too.

mammal	species	crustacean	fish
marine	adaptation	seaweed	coral

105

Term 1 Unit 2

Project 11

Speaking and listening

1. Look at the map of Jamaica and read the title. Discuss as a class:
   - What do you think this map shows?
   - What are wetlands? Have you ever seen any? Share what you know.
2. Then close your books and listen as your teacher reads this text.

> **Wetlands in Jamaica**
>
> Wetlands are areas where water covers the soil most of the time. The soil is soaked in water, which can be fresh or salty. Plants and animals have adapted to be able to live in wetlands.
>
> There are different types of wetlands in the Caribbean. The most common wetlands in Jamaica are coastal mangroves, marshes (also known as morasses), lakes and ponds. The wetlands are mainly along the coast.
>
> Coastal wetlands are important in Jamaica because they provide a habitat for fish and shellfish, which are important sources of food. The wetlands also protect the land from big waves in the sea and they filter the water on the land, which improves the quality of the water. Mangroves also prevent soil erosion.
>
> Many wetland areas have been destroyed. In the past, people thought that they were unhealthy places that brought disease. They drained the wetlands to create farming land. Now, large parts of the wetlands have been destroyed to make way for building developments.
>
>
>
> All the green areas have wetlands: St Thomas, St Elizabeth, St Ann, Kingston, St Catherine, Clarendon, Westmoreland, Trelawny and Hanover.

3. Complete this paragraph about wetlands. Do this out loud first. Can you spot any complex sentences or dependent clauses?

   1. Wetlands are places where _____.
   2. In Jamaica, the wetlands are _____, for example in _____ and _____.
   3. Wetlands are important because _____.
   4. People have destroyed many wetlands because _____.

106

4 Prepare and present a short presentation about wetlands to your class. Use these questions to help organise and structure your presentation.

- What are wetlands?
- Where are the Jamaican wetlands located?
- Why are wetlands important?
- How are wetlands being destroyed?
- What do you think about wetlands?

How to make a good presentation:
- Speak clearly and loud enough for everyone to hear.
- Use expression to make it sound interesting.
- Use an appropriate tone to suit the purpose. Is it an important point you are making or do you want to entertain and make people laugh?
- Sequence your main points in order.

Word builder

Vocabulary box

alien	erosion	mangrove	shellfish
coastal	flamingo	marsh	shrimp
crocodile	islands	morass	species
drain	lagoon	mudflat	threaten
earn	lake	pond	wetland
endemic			

1. Read all of the words by yourself. If you are not sure what a word means, use a dictionary to look it up.

2. Choose five words from the vocabulary box and write a sentence for each one.

3. There are some of the words of the vocabulary box jumbled up (anagrams) below. Can you work out what the words are?

sionero	rimpsh	codilecro	noogal	sndalis
ssarom	groveman	ingomfla	ishfellsh	

4. Choose three words from the vocabulary box and write an anagram puzzle for a partner to solve.

5. Write your own definitions of the words wetland and coastal. First try to work out what the words mean, then check in a dictionary.

> Don't copy the definitions from a dictionary. Read the dictionary definition and make sure you understand it. Then write your own definition.

Project 11 – Where are the wetlands?

Let's read

1. Find the Black River Morass on a map of Jamaica.
2. Carlene and her group recently completed a project on the wetlands of Jamaica. They want people to understand how important the wetlands are and why alien species of plants and fish can threaten the wetlands. Read this report about the project.

Black River Morass

Carlene Cumberbatch and her team recently won the Wetlands Day Awareness Competition. They created a poster and made a presentation about the Black River Morass in Jamaica.

The Black River Morass (or the *Great Morass* as it is also called) is the largest freshwater wetland in Jamaica. It is made up of lagoons, islands, tidal marshes, mudflats and mangroves. It is home to birds, crabs, fish, shrimps and crocodiles.

In their presentation, Carlene and her team explained the importance of the Great Morass. They said that there are several species of plants and animals that only live in this part of the world. These are endemic to Jamaica. They told us that this area was also the only place where the flamingo still nests. They also explained that some alien plants and fish had invaded the area and were killing off endemic species of plants and fish. Local people earned a living by fishing for shrimps and fish. Carlene concluded by saying, "We are worried that local people will not be able to earn a living if these alien species are allowed to live in the Great Morass." She said that she hoped the presentation had made people more aware of the problems facing the area.

Everyone applauded Carlene and her team for their work.

Black River Morass

Alien species threatening the Great Morass

red-claw crayfish	This crayfish eats the smaller crayfish and shrimp that Jamaicans enjoy so much.
suckermouth catfish	This fish attacks local fish.
paperbark tree	This tree grows everywhere leaving no space for indigenous trees.
water hyacinth	This plant clogs up the waterways.

Problems affecting the Great Morass:
- alien species of plants and vegetation
- pollution
- tourism

3 Answer these questions.

1. Where is the Black River Morass?
2. Give another name for this wetland.
3. Name four types of animals that live in this area.
4. What threatens the endemic plants and animals of the wetland?
5. What other problems affect the Morass?
6. What will happen if the wetlands are not protected?
7. Would you like to visit the Great Morass? Give a reason for your answer.

4 Work with a partner to find and point to the following features in the text and discuss how these features help the reader:
- title
- pictures
- diagram
- labels
- table/chart
- bullet points.

5 The words **alien** and **endemic** are antonyms (words that mean the opposite of each other). Find them in the text and discuss them with your partner. What do the words mean? Check your ideas using a dictionary.

Research and study skills

Do you think Carlene has done a good job with her project? Discuss with your partner what she did well in her project, what you would improve if you were writing it and whether there is anything you would like to find out more about.

Grammar builder

> **Look and learn**
>
> When we write words in **direct speech**, we use the exact words that someone used. We put these words inside quotation marks.
>
> For example:
>
> "The paperbark tree is a threat to the wetlands of Jamaica", said Carlene.
>
> If we report what Carlene said, we would not use quotation marks and we would write the sentence like this:
>
> *Carlene said that the paperbark tree is a threat to the wetlands of Jamaica.* This is called **reported speech**.

1. When would you use direct speech, and when would you use reported speech? Discuss your ideas with a partner. Decide whether it would be better to use direct or reported speech in the examples below.

    1. You want to tell somebody what happened but you can't remember the exact words that were said.

    2. You want to write what someone said but you only have room for a summary.

    3. You need to write down what someone else said in their exact words.

    4. You want to write down what someone said but you think you could say it more clearly.

2. Find four sentences in reported speech in the third paragraph of the text *Black River Morass* on page 109. Rewrite each sentence in direct speech with the correct punctuation.

3 These sentences are in direct speech, but the punctuation is not correct. Rewrite the sentences correctly.

1 "The Black River Morass is the largest freshwater wetland in Jamaica, said Carlene."

2 There are birds, crabs, shrimp and crocodiles in the mangrove explained the teacher.

3 "The red-claw crayfish eat the small crayfish and shrimp that we catch, said the fisherman.

4 The Black River Morass is in the parish of St Elizabeth explained the tour guide.

4 Look at the phrases in the speech bubbles and write them in reported speech.

- There are different types of wetlands in the Caribbean.
- I love jerk chicken!
- Mangroves prevent soil erosion.
- I found the information in the index.

Project 11 – Where are the wetlands?

Let's write

Task

You are going to write three paragraphs about a wetland in Jamaica. Think about all the different texts that you have read in this unit and decide what sort of text you would like to use as a model.

> **ICT opportunity**
>
> Search the internet for information about other wetlands in Jamaica. Are there any articles online that help you to learn more about a specific wetland? Is there an agency that can be emailed for more information?

Plan

1. Research wetlands in Jamaica. Then plan your paragraphs. Decide what you want to cover in each paragraph using a mind map or a diagram. Once you have your paragraph ideas, make sure your subheadings clearly describe the content.

```
            ┌──────────────────────────┐
            │ The … [name of wetland]  │
            └──────────────────────────┘
                   /            \
   ┌───────────────────────┐   ┌────────────────────────┐
   │ Plants and animals that│   │ Threats to the wetland │
   │  live in the wetland  │   │                        │
   └───────────────────────┘   └────────────────────────┘
```

2. Now you have decided on the details of what will be in your paragraphs, write a topic sentence for each one.

Write

3 Draft your paragraphs. Start with your topic sentence and write another three sentences for each paragraph. Try to write long and short sentences. Use direct speech if you are quoting what someone has said. Remember that you can make longer sentences by connecting clauses with *and*, *but*, *or* and *because*. Include at least one *because* sentence to explain why something is happening to or in the wetland.

4 As a class create a checklist for your writing. What will you need to include?

5 Use the checklist to edit and improve your writing.

Evaluate

6 Evaluate your writing. Write these sentences into your notebook:

I am really pleased with my writing because _____. I would like to improve my writing by _____.

Project 12

Speaking and listening

1. Discuss the following questions as a class.
   - What do you know about giraffes?
   - Do you know where they live?
   - Can you guess what they eat?
2. Listen as your teacher reads a poem called *Giraffes*, by Mary Ann Hoberman.
3. Find the poem online and write it down carefully.

_____

_____

_____

_____

_____

_____

_____

_____

_____

_____

4. Read the poem aloud. Can giraffes really fly? What name do we give this type of figure of speech? Discuss with your partner why you think it has been used here.

115

5. Prepare and present a presentation about giraffes or another animal that lives in grasslands. Think about the following:
   - What is the animal called?
   - What does the animal look like?
   - Where does the animal live?
   - What does the animal eat?
   - Do you know an interesting fact about your chosen animal?
   - What is your favourite thing about your chosen animal?

ICT opportunity

- Use ICT to research your chosen grassland animal.
- Use ICT to support your presentation. Perhaps you could display or show pictures of your chosen animal or key facts you have found.

Word builder

Vocabulary box

carnivore	herbivore	lion	rainfall
cheetah	hunter	omnivore	stealth
continent	hyena	predator	vulture
giraffe	jackal	prey	zebra
grasslands			

1. Read the words in the vocabulary box aloud. Then find the words that you think are the names of animals.

2. As a class, discuss techniques that help you read and understand an unknown word. Make a list, for your teacher to scribe.

3. Work on your own or in pairs to create a poster titled *How to Read an unknown word*.

4. Discuss these words with your partner. What do you think they mean? How can you tell?

   1. grassland, rainfall

   2. carnivore, herbivore, omnivore.

5. Choose six words from the vocabulary box. Make a glossary of the words and write down what you think they mean first. Then look them up in the dictionary to check them. What sort of book could you find your glossary in?

Let's read

1 Read the headings and subheadings in the magazine article. Then read the information in the box with your partner. Tell each other what this article is all about.

Living things on the savannah

The grasslands in the continent of Africa are called *the savannah*. The savannah is home to a huge variety of living things, including many kinds of plants and animals.

Plants of the savannah

Perhaps unsurprisingly, the grasslands of Africa are home to many different kinds of grass. However, the savannah also has other plants too, like the acacia, locustberry and baobab trees. They provide shelter and food to some of the animals that call the savannah their home.

Animals of the savannah

Like in other habitats, the animals in the savannah can be grouped as herbivores, carnivores and omnivores. Some of the most famous savannah animals are herbivores, including zebras, giraffes and African elephants. They use their different sizes to eat plants from the ground up to the tallest treetops!

Some savannah birds, like ostriches and grey cranes are omnivores, feeding on plants, insects and small animals such as frogs.

One of the best-known African savannah animals, however, is the lion. These carnivores hunt and eat many of the herbivores and omnivores. Cheetahs and hyenas are also savannah carnivores.

Grasslands around the world

The word *savannah* is usually used to describe grasslands in Africa. Other continents give different names to their areas of grassland. In the United States of America, grasslands are called *the prairies*. In South America, they are called *the pampas* and in Europe and Asia they are called *steppes*. Every continent of the world has grasslands except for Antarctica, because of its low rainfall.

Zebras, like giraffes, are herbivores.

Project 12 – Which animals live in the grasslands?

Research and study skills

Use a table to make three lists of some of the animals that live on the grasslands of Africa. Give each list or column in your table a single word heading. Which would be the most sensible headings to use?

2. Write answers to the questions below in your notebook:

   1. Read the first sentence of the *Plants of the savannah* subheading again. Why does it begin with "perhaps unsurprisingly"?

   2. Name two animals in the savannah that eat plants.

   3. What do birds that live on the grasslands eat?

   4. What do the carnivores in this article eat? Write your answer as a full sentence, giving one example.

3. 1. Give three more names that grasslands are known by.

   2. Why do you think grasslands might have different names in other parts of the world? Discuss your ideas with your partner.

ICT opportunity

Research different habitats on the internet. Do the texts about habitats all have the same purpose? What text features can you identify that help the reader?

Grammar builder

> **L👀k and learn**
>
> **Nouns** are the names of people, places and things:
> For example: *zebra, tree, grass, Africa, food, lion.*
> We can add **adjectives** to create **noun phrases**. These make your writing more interesting!
> For example: the *strong, fierce lion, tall trees, long, green grass.*

1 Write a noun phrase for each noun in the box.

| beach | giraffe | desert | plastic bottle | rainforest | stream |

2 Underline the noun phrase in each sentence.

1 Bottles polluted the beautiful, vast ocean.

2 Strong, fierce lions hunted on the grasslands.

3 The large, colourful flock of birds flew across the sky.

4 The water trickled over the large, sharp rocks.

5 The turtle swam easily through the turquoise, gleaming sea.

6 Tall, graceful palm trees grew along the ocean shore.

Project 12 – Which animals live in the grasslands?

Let's write

Task

You are going to write a story about the ocean and pollution. Discuss your ideas as a class.

- Who could the characters be? What will your characters look like? Write down some words to describe them.
- Where will the story take place? What will happen in the story?
- Where will the story take place? Use some adjectives, similes and metaphors to describe the setting.
- What will the problem be? How will it be solved?
- How will the story end?

If a turtle eats some plastic, it will get ill.

What can we do to solve this problem?

121

Plan

1. Plan your writing.

Character(s)	Setting	Problem	How the problem is solved	Ending

2. Draft your story. Remember to include paragraphs.

Write

3. Write your story in your best handwriting.

Evaluate

4. As a class, create a checklist for your story.

5. Re-read your story. Use the checklist to edit and improve your writing.

6. Evaluate your writing; write these sentences in your notebook:

   I am really pleased with my writing because _____.

   I would like to improve my writing by _____.

Term 1 Unit 2 Review and assessment

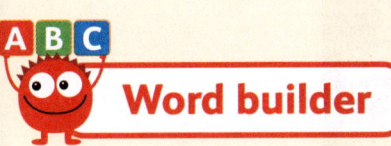

Word builder

1 Make as many words as you can from the following words:

Antarctic: _____

Africa: _____

Jamaica: _____

Wetlands: _____

2 Read this acrostic poem about the Black River Morass in Jamaica. Use your knowledge of word building to answer the questions.

> Marshes, mangroves and mudflats
> Only nesting place for flamingos
> Rare indigenous plants and animals inhabit
> Alien plants and animals must not invade
> Shrimps and crabs in abundance
> Such is the importance of the Black River Morass to Jamaica!

1 Explain what a *mudflat* is.

2 Explain what *inhabit* means.

3 An *invasion* happens when animals, plants or people take over a place that belongs to someone or something else. What does *must not invade* mean? Is it a good or a bad thing?

4 *Abundant* means *a lot of*. What does *in abundance* mean?

123

Term 1 Unit 2

3 Make a sentence in which you compare the two birds shown in the photographs. Use the word *big* in the correct form in your comparison.

4 Change the underlined words in this sentence into nouns.

1 Have you seen the new housing <u>develop</u> near the lagoon?

2 Go to the tourist office if you need <u>inform</u> about Jamaica.

Let's read

1 Read the descriptions of wetlands and deserts. Then copy and complete the table of information in your notebook.

Wetlands

Wetlands are areas where water covers the soil most of the time. Mangrove trees and other types of plants grow in the wetlands. The mangroves provide a habitat for fish, birds and animals such as crocodiles.

In the Caribbean the wetlands are mostly around the coast. The wetlands protect the land from big waves in the sea, prevent soil erosion and filter the water on the land.

Deserts

Deserts are areas where there is very little rainfall. The area is covered in sand and is very dry and hot during the day and sometimes very cold at night.

Some islands in the Caribbean are desert islands. There are sand dunes and sandy beaches. Palm trees, cacti and small scrubs grow on these islands and provide a habitat for iguanas and birds. Crabs and fish live in the surrounding sea.

	Land	Animals	Plants
wetlands			
deserts			

Review and assessment

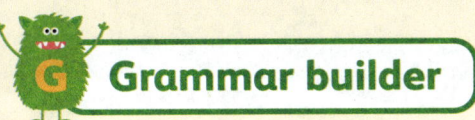 **Grammar builder**

1. Join these sentences with *because, but, and* or *so*.

    1. Canada is usually very cold. Haiti is usually quite hot.

    2. Crocodiles live in Jamaica. Flamingos live in Jamaica.

    3. Many tourists visit Jamaica every year. It is a beautiful place with lots of sunshine.

2. Write this sentence in direct speech with the correct punctuation.

    The tourist said that she enjoyed her visit to the Soufriere Hills Volcano.

    Start like this: *The tourist said, "I …,*

3. 1. Who has punctuated the sentence below in the best way, Jordan or Jonathan? Explain your choice.

    2. How would Jonathan's answer change if the word *exclaimed* was replaced by the word *stated*?

    Jordan: "This machine harvests more sugar cane in a day than fifty men with machetes can in a week", exclaimed Mr Barrett as he watched the demonstration video on the computer!

    Jonathan: "This machine harvests more sugar cane in a day than fifty men with machetes can in a week!" exclaimed Mr Barrett as he watched the demonstration video on the computer.

 **Let's write**

- Write two paragraphs about a place you have visited or you would like to visit. In your description say:
    - where the place is
    - what the place looks like
    - why people go there
    - which plants and animals you can see there.
- In your writing, demonstrate that you:
    - can write complete sentences with the correct punctuation
    - can connect ideas and sentences in your paragraphs
    - can spell the words that you use correctly.

Don't forget to check and edit your work before you hand it in for assessment!

125

TERM 2 Unit 1

Project 13

Speaking and listening

1. What special foods do you like for breakfast?
2. Listen to your teacher read the poem below. Then read it with your partner.
3. Have you ever baked anything? What happens to you when you mix the ingredients or when you knead them together? Is it the same as for Granma in the poem?
4. This poem is written in Jamaican Creole (JC). Try to say the poem in Standard Jamaican English (SJE). Which version do you prefer? Why?

I love Johnnie bake

I love Johnnie bake,
I love Johnnie bake
My mout water
wen I think of Johnnie bake
I in de kitchen
Wen Granma make Johnnie bake

Wen she grate coconut
to put in Johnnie bake
I eat de sweet, sweet bits
too small to grate.
She warn meh about belly-ache;
but I cahn help it,
I really love Johnnie bake.

She kneading de flour
an she whole body shake
I near de oven.
where she bake Johnnie bake,
looking at how she cuff
de dough flat;
and I cahn get enough
of Johnnie bake.
Nothing new!
I love Johnnie bake
I LOVE JOHNNIE BAKE!

by John Lyons

Project 13 – Special food

Word builder

> **Vocabulary box**
>
> | bake | fry | kitchen | prickly |
> |---|---|---|---|
> | coconut | grate | knead | sweet |
> | chunk | ingredients | nothing | whole |
> | dough | juice | occasions | |

1 Read the words with your partner. If you do not know all the words, try to work out their meanings from the way they are used in the poem. Write down the meanings you have guessed, then look them up in a dictionary.

2 Make a list of all the words that have something to do with cooking or preparing food.

3 Write the following words in your notebook and break them up into syllables. This will help you to say the words aloud and also to spell them.

> coconut   ingredients   occasion   prickly   kitchen

4 Use words from the vocabulary box to complete these sentences.

   1 What do I need to make callaloo? Do you have a list of _____?

   2 You can fry breadfruit, but we like to _____ it in the oven.

   3 I am so hungry. I have had _____ to eat all day!

   4 My dad makes jerk pork on special _____.

127

5 Say these words aloud:

| knead | dough | whole |

1. What letter is silent in each word?
2. Practise spelling the words.
3. Do you know any other words with silent letters? Work with a partner to complete the table below.

Words with a silent /k/	Words with a silent /w/	Words with a silent /b/
know	write	climb

Let's read

A special day

Gabrielle opened her eyes just as her alarm clock started to beep. It wasn't the harsh, loud that had awakened her, though. It was a smell. A sweet, delicious smell of something frying. Gabrielle knew that smell- it was her dad's johnny cakes! She sprang quickly from her bed and raced down the stairs.

As she ran into the kitchen, her dad scooped her up into a big hug. "Happy birthday, Gabrielle!" Dad smiled. "I can't believe you're eleven today!" Gabrielle laughed as she tried to wriggle out of his arms. She was so excited about the amazing smell that she had forgotten it was her birthday today! "I made johnny cakes for the special occasion, because I know they are your favourite." said her dad. Gabrielle ate the johnny cakes with her dad and brother Jayden. They were so soft and golden, Gabrielle thought happily. "Don't eat too many," said Dad, "or you won't be hungry for your party later!"

That afternoon, Gabrielle's family came for her birthday party. They brought her lovely gifts, and the house was decorated with balloons. Gabrielle felt very lucky to have such a wonderful birthday- especially the food! Grandma brought her famous savoury beef patties. Her Auntie Marcia made spicy, mouth-watering jerk chicken. Gabrielle and Jayden ate the chicken with her Uncle Kenneth's fluffy, tender roasted breadfruit. It was all fantastic!

At the end of the party, Dad turned off the lights and brought out a cake with eleven candles. Gabrielle's family sung as Dad brought the cake to her. In the light of the candles, she could see the beautiful cake, covered in sweet yellow icing. She closed her eyes and decided on a wish. As she blew out the candles, she thought to herself "I wish the food could be this amazing on every birthday!".

1 Read the text and answer the questions below.

1 Read the second sentence of the text again. What does **awakened** mean?

2 Why did Gabrielle's dad make johnny cakes for breakfast? Give two reasons.

3 What song do you think Gabrielle's family sing to her? Do you know the words to this song?

4 Did Gabrielle have a good birthday? Explain how you know.

Remember

Antonyms are words that mean the opposite of each other. For example, **hot** is an antonym of **cold**.

2 Make a list of eight adjectives that are used to describe food in this text. Are they all positive words? Think of antonyms for four of the words on your list.

3 How important is food to our celebrations and special days? Write a paragraph sharing your opinion. Use ideas from the story to help you.

Grammar builder

> **Look and learn**
>
> **Adverbs** are words that describe verbs and explain how something is done. For example:
>
> slowly quickly carefully gently firmly thoroughly cautiously
> excitedly greedily hungrily gracefully mysteriously strangely
> dangerously happily enthusiastically patiently

1. Work with a partner or in small groups to create a list of as many adverbs as you can. You could make a poster with adverbs to display in the classroom.

2. Read the instructions below. Identify the adverbs and copy them in your notebook.
   1. Gently, sift the flour with the baking powder.
   2. Rub the butter firmly into the flour until it makes crumbs.
   3. Add the water slowly until the mixture becomes a ball of dough.
   4. Thoroughly knead the dough and then divide equally into little balls.
   5. Carefully fry the little balls in oil.

3. Copy out these sentences and add an appropriate adverb.
   1. _____, I helped to sift the flour.
   2. I waited for the cakes to bake _____.
   3. My little brother _____ gobbled up the cakes.
   4. Very _____ the cakes were all eaten.
   5. _____, the dog licked the crumbs off the floor.

Project 13 – Special food

Let's write

Look and learn

A **simile** describes a noun by comparing it to something else, usually using the words **like** or **as**. For example:

The coconut was as hard as a rock.

The mango was bright yellow like the sun.

A **metaphor** describes a noun by comparing it to something else. For example:
The coconut ice cream was a sticky blob of snow.
The mango was a round yellow ball of sunshine.

Task

You are going to describe two foods, making one of them sound tempting and the other sound disgusting. Then you will write a poem about food.

Plan

1 Choose two foods to describe.

   1 Draw the foods.

   2 Write down four to five adjectives around each food to describe them. Use a thesaurus to find exciting words.

   3 Choose the best adjectives to make one food sound delicious and the other food sound disgusting. Write two sentences to describe each food.

   4 Write a simile or metaphor to describe each food. Add the simile or metaphor to the descriptions.

   5 Read the descriptions to your partner. Tell your partner one thing he or she did really well and one thing he or she could improve.

I love mangoes

I love mangoes
because they are delicious
because they are sweet
because they are juicy
because they are healthy
because they are stringy
I love mangoes
Even the bits that get stuck in my teeth!

Term 2 Unit 1

Write

2 Write a poem about a fruit or a meal that you enjoy.

1 Think about what the food tastes like and how you eat it.
- Remember to choose adjectives that help the reader understand why you like it.
- If you are describing something that happens all the time, what tense should you use?

2 Use this writing frame to get started:

> I ....
>   because ....
>   because ....
>   because ....
>   because ....
>   because ....
> I ....
> ....!

Use your senses when you write a poem. Think about what you see, feel, taste, smell and hear.

ICT opportunity

Use an online thesaurus to find synonyms of adjectives that you already know. For example: *delicious – mouth-watering, delectable, scrumptious.*

Note that adjectives make descriptions more interesting. For example: *a pineapple* – a ripe, juicy pineapple, *a meal* – a delicious, healthy meal.

Evaluate

3   Use the "Editor's checklist" to write down one thing you did well in your writing and one thing you would like to improve next time.

Editor's checklist

Check your poem against this checklist. You do not have to do everything in the checklist but you do need to be able to explain why not doing something in the checklist makes your poem better.

- Did you use adjectives that made the food sound tempting?
- Did you use your senses to describe the food?
- Did you use the present simple tense to describe something that happens all the time?
- Did you punctuate your poem correctly?

Project 14

Speaking and listening

1. Listen to your teacher read the poem and then read it aloud.

Fruits

Mangoes
and ripe bananas
jelly coconut
and pomegranates
jackfruit
and stinking toe
June plum
and naseberry
sweetsop
and soursop
tamarind
and jimbeli
cane juice
and coolie plum

star apple
and custard apple
navel orange
and wild cherries

fruits everywhere
brimming with life
spread out in front
of market women
buy some
and experience delight.

by Opal Palmer Adisa

2. Have you heard of all these fruits before? Discuss with a partner.
3. With your partner, discuss what fruits you like to eat.
4. Pick a fruit. Use adjectives to describe the fruit to your partner without telling them the name of the fruit. Can you partner guess which fruit you are describing?
   - What does it look like?
   - What does it taste like?
   - What does it smell like?
   - What does it feel like?
   - What sound does it make when you bite into it?

Remember ☆☆☆

An **adjective** describes a noun and provides more information about it. For example: *green, crispy, crunchy, sweet, delicious, tasty*.

5. Make an artwork which describes a fruit that you like. You can paint or draw a picture, make a collage or make the fruit from clay, wire or paper.

Then display your fruit artwork and describe how you feel about it. You can also ask others in the class to suggest words to describe the fruit.

Word builder

Vocabulary box

directions	coconut	jackfruit	character	plum
playscript	pomegranate	jimbilin	banana	cherries
stage	spice	stinking toe	apple	naseberry
wrap	tourist	vendor	sweetsop	soursop

1. Read the words in the vocabulary box aloud. Divide the words into syllables if you find them difficult to read or pronounce. For example: *cha/rac/ter* or *pom/e/gran/ate*.

2. Sort the words into two columns in your notebook: *Fruits* and *Everything else*. You should know which are fruits from the poem you just read.

3. Write down the names of the fruits in the vocabulary box in alphabetical order.

4. If you already know the meaning of a word in the *Everything else* column, write it down. If you are not sure, keep reading and see whether you can work out any of the meanings from the way the words are used. The next activity may help you with some words.

L👀k and learn

Sentences give us clues about the meanings of words. If you are not sure what a word means, read the whole sentence again, carefully.

For example: *We serve the chicken jerk in a **wrap**.*

What does *wrap* mean?

Clues from the sentence: Something in which you serve food; something that you fold around something (to wrap).

Answer: Something that you wrap around food to serve it.

5. Read these sentences and work out what the bold word in each sentence means. Use the clues in the sentence.

   1. There are lots of **vendors** at the market. They sell food and clothing.
   2. Please can you give me some **directions**? I am not sure how to act this scene from the play.
   3. Many **tourists** arrive by cruise ship to visit our beautiful island.
   4. There are four main **characters** in this play – a vendor, two tourists and another person at the market.

Project 14 – At the market

Let's read

1. Imagine you meet some tourists who want to taste some good Jamaican food. What would you suggest?
2. Look at the way the text below is arranged and find:
   1. the names of the characters in the text
   2. the instructions that tell the characters what to do.

> **Look and learn**
>
> **Playscripts** look different to stories. Look at the names of the characters on the left. These usually start with capital letters and are sometimes followed by colons (:). There are also stage directions – usually in brackets and in italic typeface.

A Jamaican lunch

Scene:
Lunch time in Kingston. Some tourists walk up to a street vendor at a market place. A passer-by is standing next to a vendor at the market. The vendor is preparing jerk chicken on an open barbecue.

TOURIST 1: *(rubbing her stomach)* I usually have lunch at 1 o'clock. I'm feeling hungry.

TOURIST 2: Me too. Let's get something from this market.

VENDOR: *(calling to the tourists)* Hello-o. Yuh look hungry. Is lunch time now enuh. Eat some jerk chicken fi lunch. A de bes'.

PASSER-BY: I'm having some jerk chicken. Try it man?

TOURIST 1: Jerk? What's that?

VENDOR: Chicken seasoned wid good herbs and spice. I mek dat myself. Real good and spicy. Serve up wid a slice of hard dough bread – yu cyan want betta dan dat.

TOURIST 2: *(looking doubtful)* Um … is it hot?

VENDOR: Yea sure. Fresh off the fire.

TOURIST 1: OK. We'll try some, thanks.

VENDOR: Be ready in jus' 3 minutes.

(A few minutes later …)

VENDOR: Here you go. Careful, now, it hot. Now mind yuh sit down nicely and enjoy it. Just open yuh mouth wide and take a beeg bite, is the bes' way.

(The tourist sits down and takes a big bite. He smiles.)

TOURIST 2: It's very good … but it's quite HOT! My eyes are watering!

(The tourist's face turns red. He blows his nose and wipes his eyes.)

VENDOR: Yes, mon. Mi tell yuh it hot. See some more napkin here.

PASSER-BY: Mind yuh eyes now. Don' rub dem. Yuh don't wan no spice in yuh eyes.

TOURIST 1: Thank you. It is delicious though.

TOURIST 2: *(coughing)* May I have some cold water please?

VENDOR: Here yuh are.

TOURIST 2: *(smiling, trying to reply in Jamaican Creole)* Tanks, mon. I think my mouth will be hot for the rest of the day – but dat was good.

(Vendor chuckles. Tourists move off.)

3 Discuss the language used in the playscript in pairs.

  1 In what tense is the sentence "I usually have lunch at 1 o'clock."?

  2 Who spoke Jamaican Creole (JC) in the play? Who spoke Standard Jamaican English (SJE)?

  3 What do you think about the language that each character uses in the play? Is it appropriate for each person? Why or why not?

  4 How can you tell what the characters are thinking and feeling? Is it easier or harder than if you were reading a story? Do you have to guess more?

  5 Make an oral summary of what happened in the play. Use five or six sentences and share it with your partner.

  6 What did you like about your partner's summary? Did he or she miss out anything important? Tell your partner one good thing about the summary and one thing you think he or she could improve next time.

4 Work in small groups. Read the text aloud with as much expression as possible. Remember to follow the stage directions. Think about:

  - what each character is thinking when he or she speaks
  - whether any gestures help to make what is happening clearer.

Grammar builder

Look and learn

What is the difference between direct speech and reported speech? Look at the way we write a statement in direct speech in a playscript and in a story. Then look at how we write this statement in reported speech.

- Look at the verbs.
- Look at the pronouns.
- Look at the punctuation marks.

Direct speech in a playscript	Direct speech in a story	Reported speech
TOURIST 1: I usually have lunch at 1 o'clock. I'm feeling hungry.	"I usually have lunch at 1 o'clock. I'm feeling hungry," said Tourist 1.	Tourist 1 said that she usually had lunch at 1 o'clock. She was feeling hungry.
VENDOR: Yes, mon. Mi tell yuh it hot. See some more napkin here.	"Yes, mon. Mi tell yuh it hot. See some more napkin here," said the vendor.	The vendor agreed and reminded him he had already said it would be hot. He offered him a napkin.

1 Work in pairs or small groups. Study the sentences in the box above and explain how the sentences are different.

- What type of language is the vendor's line reported in? Why do you think this is?

140

Project 14 – At the market

2   These sentences are from the playscript. Write the sentences in reported speech, starting with the given words.

   1   PASSER-BY: I'm having some jerk chicken.

       The passer-by said that she _____.

   2   TOURIST 1: I'm feeling hungry.

       Tourist 1 said that she _____.

   3   VENDOR: I mak' dat myself.

       The vendor said that he _____.

   4   TOURIST 2: It's very good, but it's quite HOT!

       Tourist 2 said that it _____ but it _____.

Evaluate

3   Work in pairs. Create a poster to explain direct speech and reported speech. Include some examples. Display your poster in the classroom.

Term 2 Unit 1

Let's write

Task

Work in groups. You are going to write another scene in which some tourists buy food at a local market.

Plan

1 Brainstorm your ideas first:
   - What time of day is it?
   - How many characters are there?
   - Do they all speak the same amount?
   - What sort of meals could the tourists buy?
   - How much would the meals cost?
   - What sort of people are the characters?
   - What would they say or do and how would they say or do it?

2 Think about the following:

You can use Standard Jamaican English (SJE) and Jamaican Creole (JC) in your playscript.

- When do you think each will be most appropriate?
- How will you help the audience understand what is happening using only the words people say and how they say them?

Write

3 Write a draft and role play it to check if it works well.

4 Improve the draft and read it aloud to the rest of the class.

ICT opportunity

Type your playscript on a computer. Set it out nicely with spaces. Put the stage directions in an italic typeface. Use the spellcheck on the computer to check your spelling.

Editor's checklist

When you finish your work, check it carefully.

- Did you make sure each character spoke the appropriate language?
- Did you use any time prepositions?
- Did you include the name of each speaker on the left, with a colon?
- Did you make it easy for the audience to understand what was happening?
- Did you include stage directions in italics?

Evaluate

5 Act the scene you wrote for the class or for another group. Ask them to give you some feedback.

6 Note one thing that worked well in your scene and one thing you would like to improve.

Project 15

Speaking and listening

Remember ☆☆☆

Remember to listen carefully to what others have to say. You may not agree with them, but you should show them respect and listen to what they have to say.

1. Hold a class debate/discussion about how healthy each of these meals are. Consider the following questions.

   - Which meal would you prefer and why?
   - Are these healthy meals? Explain why or why not.
   - Do they have fresh ingredients?
   - Which drink is healthier and why?

Remember ☆☆☆

Be a good listener.
- Take turns speaking.
- Listen when others are speaking.
- Share your opinion respectfully.
- Ask and answer questions.
- Encourage others to participate.

Word builder

Vocabulary box

carbohydrate	healthy	nutritious	snack
fat	legume	portion	staple
fibre	mineral	protein	unhealthy
food	nourished	salad	vitamin
group	nutrient	salty	well-nourished
fresh			

1. Work out the meanings of these words: *unhealthy, salty, nutritious, well-nourished*.

2. If there are words in the vocabulary box that you do not know, write them down and look out for them in the following text. See if you can work out each meaning before you look it up in a dictionary.

Remember ☆☆☆

To work out the meanings of words, look at the parts of the words that you already know. Some words may have a similar meaning because they are from the same word family. **Prefixes** and **suffixes** are added to words to change them into other parts of speech (for example, from a noun to an adjective). Prefixes can also change the meaning of a word. For example, the prefix *un-*, usually means *not*.

3. Break the following words into syllables: *mineral, vitamin, carbohydrate, protein*. Then say the words aloud. Look the words up in a dictionary and explain to your partner what they mean.

Remember ⭐ ☆ ☆

We can use mnemonics to help us remember how to spell a word.

A **mnemonic** is a saying, phrase or rhyme using the letters in the word in order.

For example, this phrase can help us to remember how to spell *healthy*. Each word in the phrase begins with the next letter in the word *healthy*.

healthy

eating

always

leads

to a

healthier

you

4. With your partner, choose a word from the vocabulary box and create a mnemonic to help you remember how to spell the word.

5. Write the best mnemonics on strips of paper and display them for everyone in the class to use.

Let's read

1. Last week, Dr Watkins-Baker gave Grade 5 a presentation about healthy eating. Read the report that Tamsin wrote about this.

Dr Watkins-Baker's presentation

Dr Watkins-Baker started by asking us to compare two plates of food. We had to decide which was the healthier option, which led to an interesting discussion.

Then Dr Watkins-Baker told us more about healthy eating. She said that, just like breathing, eating food is a necessary process. Eating allows your body to function and work. Your body works better when it is well-nourished. She told us that eating healthy food helps us to learn better at school!

She explained that we should eat a variety of foods every day so that our bodies get all the different nutrients that they need to function well. She also mentioned that we should not eat foods with a lot of sugar or salt. She also said that some foods have more nutrients than other foods. So if you eat a bean salad, your body will get vitamins, minerals, fat, fibre and proteins. Eating a packet of sweets will only provide lots of sugar and some fat.

Here are some of the tips she gave us:

- Learn where your food comes from. Visit a fruit farm, dairy, fishery or bakery. Try to eat food from local sources.
- Read the labels on the food that you buy so that you know what nutrients are in the food.
- Sugary cold drinks are not good for us. Drink more water.
- Eat a variety of foods every day, including foods from all food groups.
- Don't eat too much fried and salty food, for example, fried chicken or fish, and chips.
- Make your own snacks with fruits, vegetables, nuts and seeds. Too many sweets are not good for the body.
- Try to have milk, cheese, yoghurt, broccoli, salmon, peas and beans. These foods have minerals and vitamins that help to build strong, healthy bones.

Food groups	Examples of foods
Staples (carbohydrates)	pasta, rice, potatoes, cornmeal
Fruits and vegetables	mangoes, tomatoes, spinach, pumpkin
Fats and oils	butter, margarine, oil
Legumes	beans, peas, tamarind, chickpeas
Food from animals (proteins and fats)	milk, meat, fish, chicken, eggs

2. Use the text to answer the following questions. Write your answers in full sentences.

   1. Why do we need to eat food?
   2. What kinds of food should we not eat too much of? Give three examples.
   3. Look at the healthy eating tips in the report. Based on this information, do you think you have a healthy diet? Explain one way you could make your diet healthier.
   4. Do you think that Dr Watkins-Baker is an expert in healthy eating? Explain why.

3. Find the row of the table in the text called "Legumes". Use it to answer the following questions.

   1. What are three examples of legumes?
   2. What kinds of living things do legumes come from?
   3. Write your own definition of a legume.

4. Think about snacks that are healthy to eat.

   1. Draw a picture of a healthy snack. Label your picture to show the foods in the snack and which group they belong to.
   2. Write a sentence to explain why your snack is healthy.

5. Make a poster containing the most important information from Tamsin's report. Use sentences, diagrams and labels to share what you have learned.

ICT opportunity

Use the internet to research healthy and unhealthy snacks.

Grammar builder

Look and learn

The word **not** changes the meaning of a sentence.

Examples:

- Sweets are good for us.
  Sweets are **not** good for us.
- I was hungry last night.
  I was **not** hungry last night.

Sometimes we have to add **do** or **did** to make a negative sentence.

Examples:

- Drink water from the river.
  Do not (Don't) drink water from the river.
  (Add **do** for an imperative.)

- I eat pineapple on Tuesdays.
  I do not (don't) eat pineapple on Tuesdays.
  (Add **do** for the present simple tense.)

- I read the label on the packet.
  I did not (didn't) read the label on the packet.
  (Add **did** for the past simple tense.)

1 Change the meaning of these sentences. Rewrite each sentence and add the word *not*. Add *do* or *did* if you need to.

   1 Sugary cold drinks are good for us.
   2 Eat sweets as a snack.
   3 I eat chips every day.
   4 Too much chocolate is good for us.
   5 It is raining today.
   6 It was very hot yesterday.

2 Work in pairs and complete the following tasks.

   1 You are trying to be healthy. Draw up a plan of things that you will and won't do to achieve this.
   2 Share your ideas with the rest of the class.

Let's write

Task

You are going to write a story about food.

Plan

1. Discuss in small groups, or as a class, different ideas for a story. Consider the following:
   - characters
   - setting
   - a problem that may occur
   - how to solve the problem.

> You could think of a setting that involves food; perhaps a kitchen, a restaurant, a market or supermarket.

2. Plan your story, using a story map.

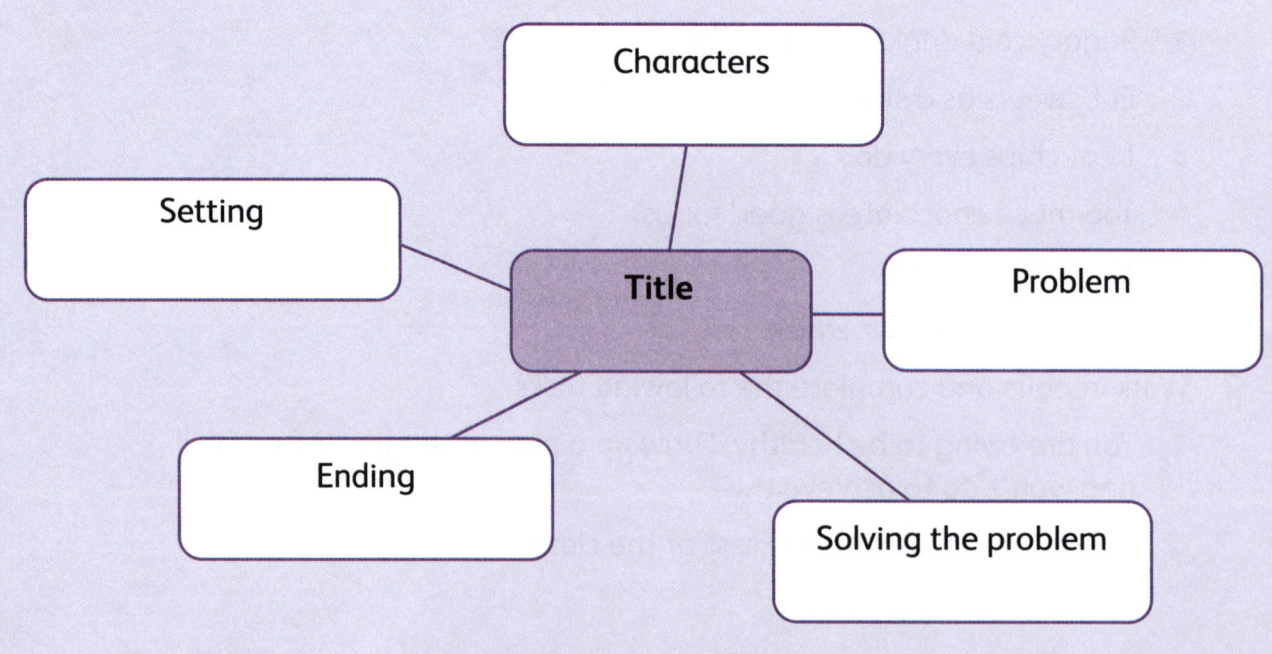

Adjectives I could use:

Adverbs I could use:

Similes or metaphors I could use:

Write

3   Draft your story. Remember to use your plan.

Evaluate

4   Work with a partner. Check each other's stories.

- Discuss each other's work and give some useful advice about how to improve the work.
- Read the notes in the "Editor's checklist".

> Be honest but kind when you check someone else's work. Your aim is to help them, not make them feel bad!

Editor's checklist

- description of characters
- description of setting
- a clear problem
- the problem has been solved
- adjectives
- adverbs
- similes and metaphors
- punctuation: capital letters, full stops, commas, speech marks

Term 2 Unit 1

Project 16

Speaking and listening

1. Close your books and listen as your teacher reads the following advertisement to you.

> **Penny's perfect pasta**
> You love pasta – right? Everyone does. But people say you shouldn't eat too much of it. So, what should you do? Well, now there's a new type of pasta you can choose – Penny's perfect pasta. It's made from legumes, so it's full of proteins and fibre. It's low in fat and has no added sugar. Try some today with your favourite sauce. You'll love the taste! Treat yourself to the best!

2. With your partner, read the advertisement again. Ask your partner three questions about the advertisement. Think about:
   - what the author is trying to do
   - what points the author makes
   - how these points help to achieve the author's aims.

   Swap roles. Let your partner read to you and ask you three different questions about the advertisement.

3. Listen to some advertisements on the radio. Make notes about one advertisement that you think is interesting.

4. Prepare a short presentation about the advertisement to the class. Tell the class:
   - what is being advertised
   - why the advertisement is interesting
   - what points the advertiser makes
   - who the advertiser is trying to appeal to
   - whether the advertisement has made you want to buy or use the product
   - whether the advertisement might make someone else buy or use the product.

152

Project 16 – Do advertisements persuade us?

Word builder

Vocabulary box

crunchiest	healthiest	lowest	taste	pasta
deserve	hottest	natural	tastiest	perfect
freshest	juiciest	spiciest	treat	

1. Read the vocabulary words to yourself. If there are words you do not know, work out the meanings from the parts of the words that you do know, before using a dictionary.

2. There are eight words in the vocabulary box that end in the same way.

   1. Can you find them? Write them in your notebook.

   2. Do you know the meanings of all eight words? What do you notice about all the meanings?

2. Work in pairs. Discuss why you think superlatives and exciting adjectives are useful in advertising.

4. Read the following sentence out loud: "The cabbage is tasty." Experiment with adjectives to make the cabbage sound more appetising:

   • Where could you add adjectives in the sentence?

   • What adjectives could you use?

Remember ☆☆☆

We use **superlative adjectives** to compare more than two things. Superlative adjectives often end in -est. For example: *This is the sweetest mango I have had this summer.* When you cannot add -est to the end, you can put **most** or **least** in front of the adjectives instead.

For example:

*It is the **most exciting** movie you will ever watch.*

*My **least favourite** food is spinach.*

This delicious, crunchy cabbage is the tastiest you'll ever eat!

153

Let's read

1 Look at the two advertisements below and quickly discuss what each is advertising.

2 Discuss the two advertisements and answer the following questions.

1 Give two reasons why you should buy *Chrissie's chocolate cookies*, according to the advertisement.

2 Can you think of any reasons why you should not buy the cookies? Why are these not in the advertisement?

3 Find four adjectives that are used in the advertisement to persuade us that the cookies are good. What do you notice about them? Why do you think the advertiser has used them?

4 Look at the picture in the cookies advertisement. Describe what it shows.

5 How does the picture help to persuade us that the cookies are good?

6 Give two reasons why you should buy *Goodies chicken*, according to the advertisement.

7 Can you think of any reasons why you should not buy the chicken? Why are these not in the advertisement?

Project 16 – Do advertisements persuade us?

8 Find four words that are used in the advertisement to persuade us that the chicken is good.

9 Which advertisement appeals to you? Why? Is it attractive and interesting? Do you think you will like the products?

L👀k and learn

Advertisers use many tricks to try and persuade us to buy things. For example:
- They use attractive pictures and big letters to make us stop and look.
- They use superlative forms of adjectives to describe the products so that we think these products are better than ordinary.

3 Compare the two advertisements. Copy and complete this table of comparison in your notebook.

	Chrissie's chocolate cookies	Goodies chicken
type of food		
nutrients		
adjectives used to describe food		
layout		simple and clear, good photograph
appeals to	anyone who likes cookies or coconut or chocolate	

Research and study skills

Work in pairs. Find another advertisement for a food product in your local newspaper. Compare your advertisement with one of the advertisements on the previous page. Think about:
- whether it makes you want to buy or use the product
- what it does better or worse than the advertisements on the previous page
- whether it uses a lot of superlatives
- what other kinds of adjectives it uses.

Grammar builder

Look and learn

Words such as **in**, **at** and **for** are prepositions that we can use to describe time. For example:

*I have lunch **at** 1 o'clock.*
*The food will be ready **in** three minutes.*
*They will be here **for** two days.*

Since, **ago**, **before**, **to**, **past**, **until**, **after**, **on** are also prepositions that tell us when something happened, is happening or is going to happen.

1 Find the prepositions in these sentences and write them in your notebook.
   1 The special offer is valid until the end of the month.
   2 I was going to eat something else before I saw the advertisement.
   3 After hearing the cookie advertisement on the radio I really wanted cookies.
   4 The advertisement has been on the radio every day since January.
   5 I have booked a table for tomorrow evening.

2 Copy the sentences and fill in the missing preposition.
   1 You must eat your lunch _____ you have a cookie.
   2 You should clean your teeth _____ eating sweets.
   3 We usually have lunch _____ half past twelve.
   4 The restaurant is open _____ 10 p.m.
   5 The market is open _____ Saturdays.

3 Work with a partner. Look at a selection of advertisements. Can you find any prepositions? Make a list in your notebook.

ICT opportunity

Look at advertisements for food products on the internet.
- Do they use adjectives?
- Do they use adverbs?
- Do you use prepositions?

Project 16 – Do advertisements persuade us?

Let's write

Background

Read this poem for fun. Then read it again, as fast as you can; it is a tongue twister.

Betty Botter's butter

Betty Botter bought some butter.
"But," she said, "the butter's bitter.
If I put it in my batter,
It will make my batter bitter.
But a bit of better butter,
That would make my batter better."

So Betty bought a bit of butter
Better than her bitter butter
And she put it in her batter
And the batter was not bitter.
So it was better that Betty Botter
Had bought a bit of better butter!

by anonymous

Task

Work in groups. Create an advertisement for *Betty Botter's butter*. Include a picture and some text to describe the butter.

Plan

1 Think about the following questions.
- What will make people buy the butter?
- Is there anything about Betty's butter that is more tempting than other butters?
- Who are you advertising to and what will be most appealing to them?

Some tips for writing advertisements:
- Make the heading big and clear.
- Use bright colours.
- Emphasise some words by using different colours and sizes of print.
- Use superlative forms of adjectives and adverbs.

Write

2 Write your draft and find or draw a picture. Use the tips above.

Editor's checklist

When you finish your work, check it carefully.

- Is the advertisement eye-catching? Do you notice it easily from a distance?
- Have you thought about who you are talking to and why they will want to buy the butter?
- Is the advertisement attractive and colourful?
- Have you made Betty's butter seem more tempting than other butters?
- Do the words on the advertisement make you want to taste or buy the product?

Evaluate

3   Work in groups and look at the advertisements you have made. Discuss these questions:

- Do any of your advertisements remind you of real adverts you have seen in shops or on television? Why?
- Which advertisement do you think a local shop could use to advertise butter?

Project 17

Speaking and listening

1. Work with a partner to make a list of phrases you would use or hear in a restaurant, fast-food venue or canteen. Discuss if these phrases are in Jamaican Creole (JC) or Standard Jamaican English (SJE). Can you say the phrases in both? When would you use Jamaican Creole (JC) and when would you use Standard Jamaican English (SJE)?

2. Work in small groups. Role play a visit to a restaurant, fast-food venue or canteen. What phrases would you use?

Word builder

Vocabulary box

advertisement	container	expiry	slogan
brand	dosage	label	suggest
calcium	endorse	product	warning
calories	energy	sell-by date	yoghurt

1 Read the words in the vocabulary box with a partner. Look up the meaning of any words you don't know in a dictionary.

2 Use words from the vocabulary box to complete these sentences.

1 My mother always buys the same b_____ of breakfast cereal because she says it is the best.

2 Many famous sportsmen and women are paid to e_____ products. This helps to sell the products.

3 There is a w_____ on the packet of biscuits. It says may contain nuts.

4 You can find information about a product on its l_____.

L👀k and learn

Prefixes are groups of letters added to the beginning of words. They can change the meaning of a word.

un- and *dis-* are prefixes that mean *not*.

un- + healthy = unhealthy, dis- + pleased = displeased

Project 17 – Food labels

3 Add a prefix to a root word to create a new word. Write down the new meaning and draw a table like the one below.

Prefix	Root word	New word	Definition
un-	healthy	unhealthy	not healthy
un-	safe		
		uncooked	
dis-	pleased		
		disapprove	do not approve
	like	dislike	

Remember ☆☆☆

If you understand part of a word, you can use this to work out the meaning.

Term 2 Unit 1

Let's read

1. The list below shows the sort of information that can be found on food packages.

    1. Complete the list as a group.
    2. Share your completed lists with your class.

    Information about:
    - where the product was made
    - the brand name of the product
    - what is in the product
    - how the product was made
    - ....
    - ....
    - ....
    - ....

2. Read the information on the following carton of milk and answer the questions.

    1. What is the brand name of this product?
    2. How much milk is in this carton?
    3. Find five words that describe what kind of milk this is.
    4. Write down the slogan on the carton that advertises the milk.
    5. Which people endorse the milk?
    6. How many calories are there in 100 ml of this milk?
    7. How many grams of calcium are there in 100 ml of this milk?
    8. Can you get all the protein you need each day by just drinking 100 ml of this milk?

Project 17 – Food labels

3. Imagine your friend does not like milk very much. Discuss with your partner whether the milk carton label would make your friend want to drink milk.

   1. What changes could you make to the label to make it more tempting?

   2. Draw a label of your own, making sure you include the same scientific facts about the milk.

Extra challenge

Imagine you are a farmer in Jamaica who wants to sell their milk. Design a carton for your milk that will make others want to buy it. Remember to include all of the information from the list on the previous page on your packaging.

Grammar builder

Look and learn

In the present simple tense, the subject of a sentence must "agree" with the verb.
Examples:

- *I like* fruit for breakfast. *They like* fruit for breakfast. **BUT**
- *He likes* fruit for breakfast. *Taryn likes* fruit for breakfast.

  "He" and "Taryn" are subjects in the third person.

In a long sentence it is often hard to decide whether the verb should be singular or plural.
Examples:

- **The mangoes** on the tree **are** not ripe yet.

  (The subject is *mangoes* which is plural, and this agrees with the plural verb *are*.)

- **Andre**, along with the restaurant manager, **creates** a new menu.

  (The text between commas is an extra part. The subject of the sentence is *Andre*, and the verb *creates* must agree with the subject.)

1. In pairs, find the subject and the verb in each sentence.
   1. Margaret, along with the owner, manages the restaurant.
   2. She, with some help from her sister, always completes her homework.
   3. Your collection of baseball cards is amazing.
   4. The children in the class are well-behaved.

2. Find the subject in the sentence and then choose the verb that agrees with the subject. Write the sentences in your notebook.
   1. The shells on the beach is / are beautiful.
   2. She like / likes plums and peaches.
   3. The children, along with their parents, play / plays football every Monday evening.
   4. He always go / goes to bed before 9 p.m.

Let's write

Ben Hughes is a well-known chef. He is on a television programme and he often talks about the importance of a healthy diet.

1. Use the template below to write a letter to Mr Hughes. Ask him to come and speak to your class about eating a balanced diet.

- Explain clearly what you would like him to do, and say where and when you would like him to speak.
- Be polite and keep the letter short and to the point.
- Remember to include useful details: time, date, venue and name of the event.

[Sender's Address]
....
....

[Date] ....
[Recipient's Name/Title] ....
[Recipient's Address] ....
....

[Salutation] ....,

Our Grade 5 class at .... is planning a .... and are hoping that you will be willing to .... } Paragraph 1: Introduce yourself and make your request.

We think it would be a great idea to hear from a chef how to .... } Paragraph 2: Explain your request in more detail.

The [event] is scheduled for .... at .... } Paragraph 3: Suggest a time and place for the talk.

We really hope that you can make it and look forward to hearing from you how to .... } Paragraph 4: Conclude the letter.

Sincerely,
....

---

2. Can you think of any other situations where writing a letter would be useful? Who has written to you? Who would you write to?

Editor's checklist

When you finish your work, check it carefully.

- Have you explained what you would like Mr Hughes to do?
- Have you included the time and date of the event?
- Have you told Mr Hughes where the event will be held?
- Have you included a date and address on the letter?
- Have you included a polite salutation?
- Is your letter neat and without any spelling mistakes?

Evaluate

3 Work with a partner. Read your partner's letter. Then pretend you are Ben Hughes. Phone your partner (who wrote the letter) and reply to the invitation, showing that you understand what the letter was about. Then swap roles.

Project 18

Speaking and listening

1. Read this interview with Sherwin Blake and find out about his career as a dietician.

Interview with a dietician

Journalist: Hello, Sherwin. Please tell us about your interesting job.
Sherwin: I am a dietician and I work in a hospital.
Journalist: How do you start your day?
Sherwin: The first thing I do is to read through the patients' charts so that I can see what the nurses and doctors have observed.
Journalist: And do you talk to the patients?
Sherwin: Oh, yes! That's very important. I talk to the patients after I have read their charts.
Journalist: Do you decide what meals they will get while they are in hospital?
Sherwin: Yes, I do. There are some people who should not have any sugar in their food. There are others who can eat only soft food some days.
Journalist: And do you see the patients after they have left the hospital?
Sherwin: Yes, I often do. Some people need to follow special diets and I help them to plan these diets.
Journalist: What did you study to be able to do this job?
Sherwin: I studied Nutrition and Chemistry at college.
Journalist: What special skills do you need?
Sherwin: You have to be patient and you have to be a good listener. You also need to be caring when you look after sick people.

2. Work in pairs. Role play the interview, following the script. Remember to use expression when you are speaking.

3. With your partner, make a list of jobs that involve working with food. How many can you think of?

4. Choose a job that involves working with food, such as a restaurant manager or a chef. Imagine you are going to interview this person. What questions would you ask about their job? Write a list.

5. Work with a partner to role play an interview with someone who works with food. One person should take on the role of the interviewer and the other the interviewee (chef, restaurant manager, shopkeeper, etc.) Then swap roles.

Word builder

Vocabulary box

chef	hygienic	seafood
diet	menu	skills
dietician	patient	special
food technologist	ready-made	train
hard-working	restaurant manager	waitress

Look and learn

Suffixes are groups of letters added to the end of a word.

-ist, -ian, -er are suffixes show *what a person does*.

For example:

paint + er = painter. A painter is someone who paints.

music + ian = musician. A musician is someone who plays music.

Note: If a root word ends in *-y*, take off the *-y* to add *-ian* or *-ist*.

For example:

pharmacy + ist = pharmacist. A pharmacist is a person who works in a pharmacy.

1 Draw a table like the one below in your notebook. Fill in the missing boxes to make words. For example: *music + -ian = musician*.

Root word	Suffix	New word
farm	-er	
wait		waiter
history	-ian	
	-ian	mathematician
geology	-ist	
science		scientist

Project 18 – Careers around food

2 What job do you think these people do? Write the job and a definition.
For example: *baker – someone who bakes (cakes, bread)*.

Job	Definition
painter	someone who paints things
waiter	
librarian	
electrician	
scientist	
cyclist	

Remember ☆☆☆

If you know part of a word, you can use this knowledge to work out the meaning.

Term 2 Unit 1

Let's read

1. Skim through the three text boxes below. Write down what you think the texts are about and why, adding a reason after the word *because*.

> **L👀k and learn**
>
> We **skim** a text quickly to get an idea of what it is about. It is a good idea to read headings and to look at pictures in the text when we do this.
>
> We **scan** a text to look for specific information when we want to answer a question about the text.

2. Work in pairs. Read the texts carefully with your partner. Ask each other questions about each text.

Chef Andre

Andre is a chef in a busy restaurant in Kingston. Andre, along with the restaurant manager, creates a new menu for the resturant. Every morning, while most people are still asleep, he goes to the market to buy fresh ingredients. When he gets back, he starts to prepare the food for lunch. After lunch, he starts on the dinner menu.

It is hard work. Chef Andre often gets home only after 11 p.m. He trained for ten years to become a chef. He says that chefs need to be patient and hard-working.

Kerry-May

Kerry-May is a food technologist. She works in a small factory that prepares the ready-made meals that people buy in supermarkets. Her job is to make sure that the meals are nutritious and that the ingredients used in the meals are fresh and properly cooked or prepared. She also makes sure that the meals are hygienically prepared. She compiles the food labels that list the nutritional content of the meals. Kerry-May studied food technology at college.

Margaret Brown

Margaret Brown is a seafood restaurant manager. She works in a restaurant in Ocho Rios. She started working as a member of the waiting staff about five years ago. She learned how to be a manager on the job – while she was working. Margaret, along with the owner, manages the restaurant. She makes sure that everything runs smoothly and that the restaurant is clean. She puts advertisements outside to tell people about special meals they can have at the restaurant.

3. Read the sentence you wrote in Activity 1. Were you right? Did the clues help?

4. Copy this table in your notebook and complete it to make a summary of the information in the texts. Scan the texts for the information that you need.

Job	Place of work	Training	What the work involves

What's your view?
Would you like to do any of the jobs from the texts? Discuss why.

G Grammar builder

Look and learn

Intervening phrases are groups of words used within a sentence; these phrases don't make sense on their own. They add more information and context to a sentence. The intervening phrase usually separates the subject and the verb. We use a comma before and a comma after the intervening phrase.

*Andre, **who is a busy chef**, designs the menus at the fish restaurant.*
   ↑   ↑   ↑

subject   intervening phrase   verb

1 Copy these sentences in your notebook and underline the intervening phrases.

1. The chef, who works in a busy restaurant, likes to fish in his spare time.
2. The baker, with his friends and family, organised a cake sale for charity.
3. The supermarket, which was very popular with locals, was closed on Monday for refurbishment.
4. The vegetables, which the children had picked, tasted delicious.
5. The market, which was very busy, sold tasty, sweet mangoes.

2 Copy these sentences in your notebook, adding commas to separate the intervening phrases.

1. The food technologist who worked at the small food factory was excited to see her meals in the supermarket.
2. Mangoes which were the chef's favourite fruit were the used to make the dessert.
3. Every morning while most people are still asleep the chef goes to the market to buy fresh fish.

3 Add an intervening phrase to each of the sentences below. Write the sentences with intervening phrases into your notebook.

1. The farmer was ploughing the field.
2. The chef was cooking a delicious meal.
3. The fisherman was going out to sea on his boat.
4. The mangoes were almost ripe.

Project 18 – Careers around food

Let's write

Task 1

1. Choose a job that involves food; it could be a baker, a chef, a farmer, a food technologist or another job of your choice.

ICT opportunity

Do some research on the internet and find out about other jobs that people do that involve food.

2. Do some research about the job; you could look in the library, on the internet or interview someone. Make some notes about the job, considering the following:
   - the job title
   - place of work
   - training needed to do this job
   - what the work involves.

```
                          what the work involves
                                    |
          place of work — job title — training needed
```

3. Write three paragraphs about the job you choose to research. Remember to include:
   - subheadings
   - a topic sentence for each paragraph
   - adjectives and adverbs
   - intervening phrases.

Task 2

1. Choose a piece of writing that you have done in this unit. It should be the piece that you like the best or the one that you think is most successful.
2. Present your writing to the class.
   - Read it aloud and then say what you like about it.
   - Say what you would do next time if you were to write it again.

Term 2 Unit 1 Review and assessment

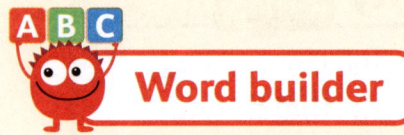

Word builder

1. Make two lists with the words in the box below. Then give each list one of the following headings: *Vegetables*, *Fruits*, *Nutrients*, *Furniture*.

coconut	protein	fibre	vitamins
apple	banana	soursop	fats
carbohydrate	naseberry	cherry	minerals

2. Choose two of these jobs. Write what each job is about.

   chef   restaurant manager   dietician   food technologist

Let's read

1. Read the advertisement for PB peanut bars and answer the following questions.

   1. What product does this advertise?

   2. Find two adjectives that describe the product.

   3. Give two reasons why you should buy a PB peanut bar, according to the advertisement.

   4. Would you buy PB peanut bar? Give a reason for your answer.

PB peanut bars
- The crunchiest, **cheapest** snack in Jamaica!
- High in proteins.
- No added sugar or salt.
- It's **healthy** and it tastes **delicious**.

GET YOUR PB PEANUT BAR TODAY.

Review and assessment

2   Read the information on the jar of jam and answer the following questions.

   1   What is the brand name of this product?

   2   How much jam is in the jar?

   3   Where is this jam made?

   4   What ingredients are there in this jam?

   5   Do you think this jam is healthy? Give a reason.

 **Grammar builder**

1   Rewrite the verbs in these sentences correctly.

   1   Shereen love pineapple jam.

   2   Do you haves a brother?

   3   My aunty cooking very good goat curry.

   4   We makes our own pineapple jam.

2   Use reported speech to write down what these tourists said about Jamaica.

   1   "We always have a good time here!" said a man.

   2   "I enjoy the chicken jerk", said a woman.

3   Make each of these statements negative.

   1   It rained yesterday.

   2   I eat sweets every day.

   3   It is hot today.

   4   Did you see the big fish?

175

4 Complete the table below by inserting the adjectives or the comparative or superlative forms of the adjectives.

Adjective	Comparative	Superlative
		calmest
	lovelier	
far		
		most
	heavier	
perfect		
fresh		
interesting		

5 Rewrite each sentence using the correct forms of the adjectives in brackets.

1. We only use the (fresh) ingredients in our restaurant!

2. I think that chicken jerk is (tasty) than chicken pie.

3. The (healthy) foods are fresh, local foods.

4. I don't like very (spicy) food.

6 Do you understand the Grammar you have practiced in this Term? Write two or three sentences in your journal about how well you understand or do not understand the following:

- how to form adjectives
- how to write reported speech
- how to use negatives

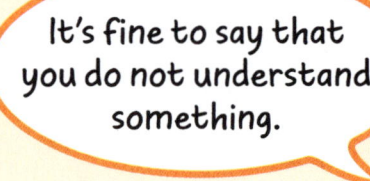
It's fine to say that you do not understand something.

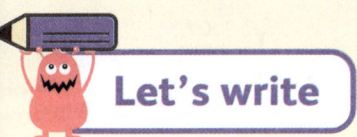

Let's write

1. Write one paragraph of six to seven sentences about one of the following topics:
   - My favourite fruit
   - My favourite meal is also good for me!
   - Make healthy choices

2. Write a short advertisement for one of the following products:
   - Mrs Peterson's perfect pasta
   - Charmaine's chocolate ice cream

In your writing, demonstrate that you can do the following:
- Choose the most appropriate words in your description and your advertisement.
- Spell words correctly.
- Check and edit your work before you hand it in for assessment.

TERM 2

Unit 2

Project 19

Speaking and listening

1. What is a parish? Discuss as a class or in small groups.

   1. In which parish do you live?

   2. Tell the class about what you know about parishes in Jamaica.

2. Look at the two maps.

This map of Jamaica was made in 1758.

Project 19 – Parishes in Jamaica

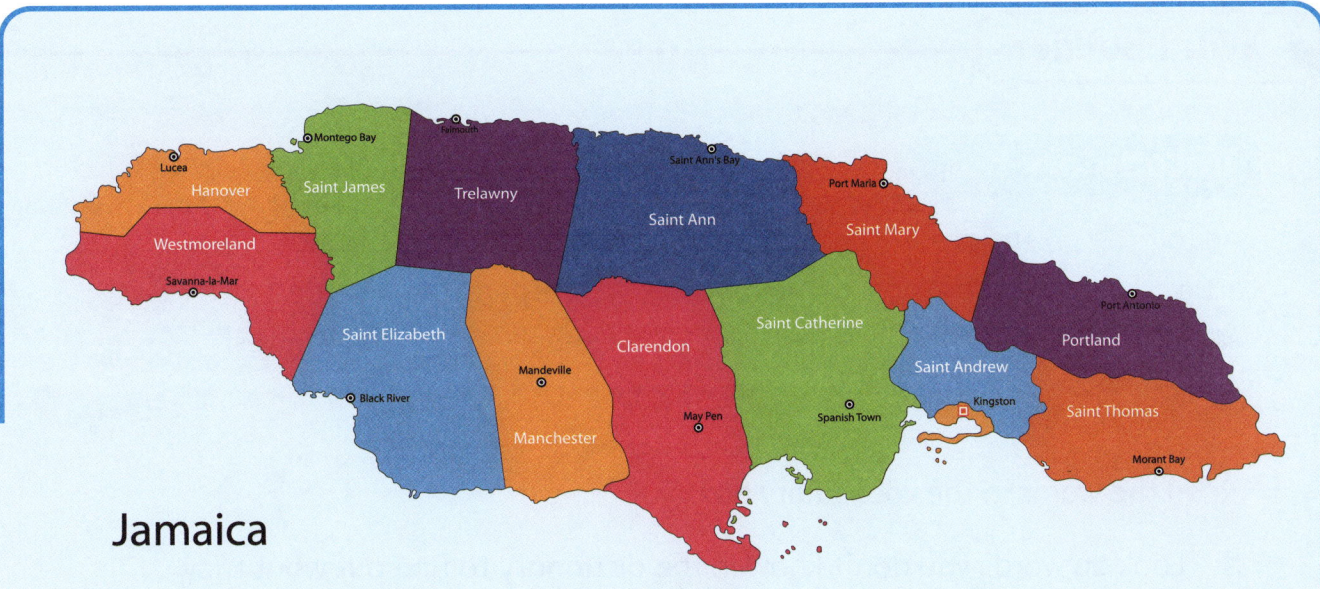

Jamaica

This is a modern map that shows the parishes of Jamaica.

1 Find the names of all the parishes in Jamaica on the modern map.

2 Look at the old map. What were parishes called then? Are any of the names still the same?

Word builder

Vocabulary box

capital	enslave	independent	parish	saint
cattle	escape	molasses	prosperous	settler
century	governor	mouth	rebellion	southwest

1 Read the words in the vocabulary box.

  1 Look up words you don't know in the dictionary to find out what they mean.

  2 Choose four words from the vocabulary box. Check the meaning in the dictionary. Then write a definition in your notebook in your own words.

Look and learn

A **synonym** is a word that means the same or something similar to another word.
Huge is a synonym of *big*.
An **antonym** is a word that means the opposite of another word.
Small is an antonym of *big*.

Remember ☆☆☆

You can use a thesaurus to find synonyms.

2 These words have meanings that are the same or similar to one of the words in the vocabulary box. Find the synonyms for the following words in the vocabulary box:

1 rich, successful

2 cows

3 run away from

4 free

3 Match the words to their antonyms.

| small |
| local |
| official |
| busy |

| calm |
| big |
| unauthorized |
| national |

4 Create a poster about synonyms and antonyms. Make your poster bright and colourful and try to include:

- a title
- examples of synonyms
- examples of antonyms.

Let's read

1. Skim the text *St Elizabeth parish* quickly and write down in one sentence what you think it is about.

> **Remember** ☆☆☆
>
> We **skim** through a text quickly to get an idea of what it is about.
> - Read the headings and look at the pictures in the text.
> - Look for names of people and places, which start with capital letters.

2. Read the text carefully with a partner.

   1. Did you get the right idea when you skimmed the text? Why do you think that is?

   2. How do you think you could practise skimming to get better?

St Elizabeth parish

St Elizabeth is a parish in the south-western part of Jamaica. The capital is Black River, which is on the mouth of the Black River.

St Elizabeth is one of the oldest parishes in the country. The first people to live in the area that is now called St Elizabeth were the Tainos. When the Spanish arrived in Jamaica, they enslaved the Taino people. The Spanish left when English settlers arrived on the island in 1655. People think that the parish was named after Elizabeth Modyfood, the wife of the first British governor of Jamaica. Some towns on the island still have Spanish names, for example Santa Cruz.

The English settlers developed the sugar cane plantations in St Elizabeth and, as a result, the parish became very prosperous. Black River became an important port on the coast. Sugar cane, molasses and trees were exported from Jamaica through this port. Other industries developed later, such as cattle farming, paper making and bauxite mining.

Many Tainos and Maroons fled to the hills of St Elizabeth because they wanted to escape from the Spanish and the English. They created their own independent communities in the hills, and built towns such as Accompong. St Elizabethans played an important role in the slave rebellion led by Sam Sharpe in 1831.

Project 19 – Parishes in Jamaica

3 Scan the text to find the answers to the following questions.

> **Remember** ☆☆☆
>
> We **scan** a text to look for specific information.
> - Read the question carefully and look for key words.
> - Find these key words in the text.

1 Where is the parish of St Elizabeth in Jamaica?

2 Who were the first people to live in this part of Jamaica?

3 Name two groups of settlers who came to live in this part of Jamaica.

4 What made St Elizabeth a wealthy place during the English occupation?

5 Why is Black River an important town in St Elizabeth?

6 Why did some Tainos and Maroons go and live in the hills of St Elizabeth?

4 Has the history of St Elizabeth parish only been positive, or have some negative things happened, too? Explain your answer in full sentences.

5 Think about the names of some of the places you know.

1 Do you know the history of any of the names? Can you guess them?

2 With your partner, discuss how you might find out more.

Research and study skills

An interesting fact about St Elizabeth is that it was the first parish to get electricity, at the end of the 19th century.

- With your partner, do some research on the internet and find two more interesting facts about St Elizabeth. Write them down in full sentences, in your own words.

- Share these facts with the class. Make sure to explain why you think your facts are interesting and share your sources.

G Grammar builder

> **Look and learn**
>
> We can use **transitional words** to join ideas, sentences and paragraphs.
>
> Here are some examples of transitional words: *because, but, so, as, also, therefore, similarly, however, in addition to.*

1. Read the sentences below. Copy the sentences into your notebook and underline the transitional word.

   1. I forgot to use punctuation in my writing because I was rushing it.
   2. I was going to research on the internet, but my computer wouldn't work.
   3. Yesterday, I went to the library so I could research my local parish.
   4. In addition to visiting the library, I have interviewed people in the community.
   5. I have enjoyed this project, however, it was very time-consuming.

2. Read the sentences below. Use a suitable transitional word to fill in the gap.

   1. I am looking forward to finding out more about my parish _____ it will be really interesting.
   2. We are going to the library _____ that we can research the local parish.
   3. I am researching the local parish with a partner _____ we will be writing our own reports.
   4. My teacher asked me to research the local parish _____ I searched the internet for useful information.

3. Work with a partner. Look for examples of transitional words in newspapers, information texts and leaflets or stories. Make a list of the transitional words you find.

Project 19 – Parishes in Jamaica

Let's write

1. Work in pairs. Find out more about your parish and write about it. Do your research online or at your local library.
   - Try to find at least six interesting facts about the parish.
   - You can also find out about famous people who lived in the parish.

Evaluate

2. Write two or three paragraphs about your parish. Remember to use a topic sentence to start each paragraph.

3. Find out who wrote the most original fact in your class.
   1. On a separate piece of paper, write the fact about your parish that you think is the most interesting. Use your own words and full sentences. Then write your name on the back.
   2. Put everyone's facts together and sort them. Who has written a fact nobody else has thought of?

Extra challenge

Make a poster with the information you have collected and use the poster to prepare a presentation for the class.

ICT opportunity

Use the internet to research about your parish.

185

Term 2 Unit 2

Project 20

Speaking and listening

1. Look at the photographs below. They all show services that local governments, like parish councils in Jamaica, provide. Describe what you see in each photograph.

2. Think about your own homes and parish, and about the places you pass on your way to school. Discuss the following questions with your teacher.
   - Who makes sure the streetlights are working?
   - Who provides a bus service?
   - Who provides the water that you get in the taps?
   - Who looks after the sports fields?
   - What important buildings are managed by the parish council?

3. As a class, discuss the roles and functions of the parish council.
4. If you had the opportunity to interview the mayor, what questions would you like to ask and why? Discuss as a class.
5. Write down five questions you could ask the mayor to find out about the roles and functions of the council.
6. Discuss what will happen if people do not use the facilities provided by local government.

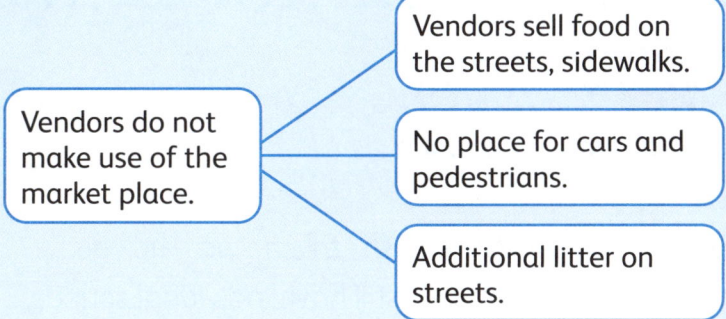

Discuss:
- What will happen if people don't use public transport.
- What will happen if people don't use bins.

Word builder

Vocabulary box

authority	garbage	prepare
breach	mayor	project
campaign	parish	receive
clear	park	street
clerk	physical	

Remember ☆☆☆

Digraphs are two letters that make one sound.
Here are some examples:

ee ea ai ay ie ue oo oa oo ar er sh th ch ng ar au

Blends and **clusters** are groups of letters that still have individual sounds.
Here are some examples:

br cr dr fr fl cl sm sn pl pr str tch

Read the diagraphs, blends and clusters and say them out loud.

Can you think of any other diagraphs, blends and clusters?

Project 20 – The roles and functions of the parish council

1. Read the words in the vocabulary box and look up the meaning of each word in the dictionary.
2. Time to be a word detective! Work with a partner. Copy each word from the vocabulary box into you notebook and underline the diagraphs, blends and clusters.
3. Choose a diagraph. How many words can you think of with this sound? Create a list in your notebook.

> Look for diagraphs, blends and clusters when you are reading unknown words to help decode them.

Let's read

Look and learn

Here is a list of text features used in non-fiction texts. These features help the reader to locate information quicker and understand the text:

- heading
- subheading
- transitional words and phrases
- diagrams
- photographs and captions.

1. Choose a non-fiction text about the local government or mayor (from the internet, books in the library or a text supplied by your teacher). Find the features listed above in the text. You could underline and label the features or make notes in your notebook. If the text does not have one or more of these features, suggest a reason for this.

2. Draw the table below in your notebook. Use a selection of non-fiction texts to fill in the table.

Feature	Purpose	Example
heading		
subheading		
transitional words and phrases		
diagrams		
photographs and caption		

What's your view?

Look at the list of features again. Do you think one of these features is more important than the others? Explain your ideas.

Project 20 – The roles and functions of the parish council

Grammar builder

> **Look and learn**
>
> **Pronouns** are words we use instead of nouns. For example:
>
> *I you he she it we you they*
>
> We can use pronouns in speech and writing, so we don't have to keep repeating the noun.
>
> Here is an example:
>
> **The teacher** asked the class to be silent. Then, **he** introduced the mayor.
>   ↑   ↑
> noun phrase   pronoun

1. Write the following sentences into your notebook and underline the pronouns. Then identify the noun each pronoun is referring to. The first one is done for you.

   1. (The mayor) visited our school yesterday. He was very interesting to listen to.

   2. The children went to the park. They were excited to try out the new play equipment.

   3. Rhona, you read the poem to the mayor beautifully, with such confidence.

   4. During the meeting, the councillors discuss the need to repair the Town Hall roof. They were all in agreement.

   5. Grade 5 visited the Town Hall on Wednesday. It was really interesting and we all had a great time.

Let's write

Task

Write or type an introduction for the mayor.

ICT opportunity

Use the internet to find out about the mayor of your local area and make notes. Find out the following:
- title
- name
- relevant personal background information (work organisation, job and experience, for example, how long they have been the mayor).

Use the internet to find examples of addresses. Read the following questions carefully.
- What do they include?
- What structure do they follow?
- What vocabulary is used?

Plan

1. As a class, create a checklist for writing your introduction. What do you need to include? Consider:
   - punctuation
   - vocabulary
   - content
   - structure.
2. Write a draft introduction for the mayor.

Write

3. Write or type up your introduction to the mayor.

Evaluate

4. With your partner, read your introduction for the mayor. Use the class checklist to edit your draft. Present your introduction to the class.

Project 21

Speaking and listening

1. The following is a discussion among a group of parish councillors. They are discussing the introduction of free Wi-Fi in the local park. Read the dialogue aloud in groups of four.

Parish councillors in discussion

Councillor 1: Some community members have requested free Wi-Fi in Green Park.

Councillor 2: Why? To use social media? I think free Wi-Fi would be more useful in government buildings.

Councillor 3: Some students go outside to do their homework in the park. Wi-Fi would be useful.

Councillor 4: And many members of the community do not have Wi-Fi at home.

Councillor 1: That's true. Maybe more students would go to the parks.

Councillor 2: Yes, and maybe they would help to take care of the parks, too.

Councillor 4: Let's conduct a survey among our community members.

Councillor 3: Yes, and let's find out what this would cost as well.

2. Role play a scene in which four councillors discuss another council matter.

   1. Choose one of these topics:
      - new library opening hours
      - free public transportation for students
      - summer art or music camp for primary school students.

   2. Think about your councillors and what their opinions will be on the topic before you start discussing it. Does every councillor have the same opinion? Consider:
      - what the changes are
      - why you want to make changes
      - what the effect of those changes will be
      - whether all the effects will be good, or if there are any reasons not to make a change.

Term 2 Unit 2

Word builder

Vocabulary box

courthouse	councillor	greeting	scare	street lights
supermarket	date	mayor	unfortunately	ice cream
wastewater	enough	paddle	waste	playground
address	fountain	safe	bin	management
because				

Remember ☆☆☆

Compound words are words that are made up of two words put together. For example:

super + market = supermarket

play + ground = playground

Some compound words have a hyphen or a gap. For example: *passer-by, street lights*

1 Read the words in the vocabulary box.

  1 Look up the meaning of any words you don't know in the dictionary.

  2 How many compound words can you find in the vocabulary box?

2 Copy the table below into your notebook. Use the compound words you have found in the vocabulary box to fill in the table.

Compound word	Individual words	Meaning	Dictionary definition
ice cream	ice + cream	frozen or cold cream	
courthouse			
supermarket			

194

Project 21 – Making changes

Let's read

1 Skim the letter. Then answer the questions on the next page.

> St Patrick's Primary School
> 23 Red Hills Road
> Kingston 8
> Jamaica
>
> 21 February

His Worship the Mayor, Councillor Conroy Wilson
Mayor of Kingston
24 Church Street
Kingston

Dear Sir,

We are writing to ask for your help. There is a park near our school where we like to play. Unfortunately, our teachers and parents will not allow us to go there now because they say it is not safe or clean.

Here are some of the problems:
1 There are not enough waste bins and the bins are also not emptied very often. As a result, the park often looks dirty.
2 There is no water in the toilets, so we cannot use them.
3 The fountain does not work anymore, so we cannot paddle there when it is hot.
4 We don't always feel safe in the park, because some of the people there scare us and ask for money and food.

We would like to invite you to visit our school and the park so that we can discuss what can be done. We acknowledge that you are very busy, but we hope that you will find the time to come and visit. We would like to help to make the park nice again.

Yours sincerely,

Grade 5

1. Who wrote the letter?
2. To whom is the letter addressed?
3. What is the letter about? Write two sentences explaining what is in the letter.

L👀k and learn

Letters are written for many different purposes. A letter to a friend or family member is usually **informal** - this means that you might:

- use contractions like *I'm* or *don't*
- call the person by their first name or nickname
- end the letter with a phrase like *Lots of love* or *See you soon!*

A letter to someone with an important job, or someone who you don't know, is usually **formal**. This means that you might:

- use longer words or phrases, like *furthermore* or *I acknowledge...*
- call the person by their full name, or a title like sir or madam
- end the letter with *Yours sincerely* (if you know the name of the person) or *Yours faithfully* (if you do not know their name)

2 Look at the letter again.

1. Is the letter written in a formal or informal style? Give two ways that you know.
2. Why have Grade 5 chosen to write this letter in this style?
3. Do you think that the mayor would reply to this letter in a formal or informal style? Why?

3 Discuss and answer these questions with your partner. Scan the letter carefully to find the information.

1. What is the address of St Richard's Primary School?
2. When was the letter written?
3. What are the four main problems in the park that are mentioned in this letter?
4. Why has the class written to the mayor? What have they asked him to do?
5. Do you think it is a good idea to write to a mayor to ask for help like this? Why or why not?

Project 21 – Making changes

Grammar builder

> **Look and learn**
> The **subject** of a sentence is the person, place or thing that the sentence is about.
> The **verb** is the action that has happened, is happening or is going to happen.

1 Read the sentences. Copy the sentences into your notebook. Choose the correct verb to match the subject.

1 The children was / were going to visit the mayor.

2 The child was / were excited to receive a letter from the mayor.

3 The teacher has / have invited the mayor to visit.

4 The teachers has / have organised an outing in the town.

5 The park is / are closed after dark.

6 The parks is / are all closed after dark.

7 I am / are going to the Town Hall tomorrow.

8 We am / are raising money to mend the school roof.

> **Look and learn**
> **Verbs** ttell us about an action or event in the **present**, **past** or **future**.
> For example:
> I <u>wrote</u> to the mayor. (past)
> I <u>am writing</u> to the mayor today. (present, something you are doing now)
> My father <u>writes</u> to the mayor quite often! (present, action that is repeated often)
> Kingston <u>is</u> the capital city of Jamaica. (present, something that is true, a fact)
> She <u>will write</u> to the mayor tomorrow. (future)

197

2 Read the sentences. Identify the verb tense in each sentence and discuss why it has been used.

1. The children went to see the mayor.
2. The children are walking to the Town Hall.
3. We asked the mayor lots of questions.
4. We collect litter at the park every week.
5. We will make posters to encourage people to put their litter in the bins.
6. The mayor is speaking to Grade 5 about his role and responsibilities.
7. My father is a night owl because he stays up late.
8. The Dunn's River Falls is in Jamaica.

Let's write

Task

Work in pairs. Write a letter to the mayor of your town asking her or him for assistance with a project.

> ### Look and learn
>
> We write letters in a certain way, so that it is easy to understand who wrote the letter, when it was written, to whom it was written, and what the letter is about.
>
> A letter should include the following:
> - the name and address of the person to whom you are writing
> - your own address
> - the date
> - a greeting (Dear Sir/Madam, Mrs Williams, Jane)
> - a subject line, which says what the letter is about
> - a closing line (Yours sincerely, Best wishes, Kind regards)
> - your name at the end.

Plan

1. Discuss the following with your partner.
   - What is the project that you will ask for help with?
   - What is the problem that the mayor can help with?
   - How will you ask for help? What words will you use?
2. Think of at least four reasons to convince the mayor to help you.
   - How could you present the reasons? Would a list be useful?
3. Explain why you think the mayor is the best person for the job.

Write

4. Write your letter using the layout template provided on the next page.

Use the correct format when you write a formal letter.

.... your address

.... the date

.... }– the address of the person to whom you are writing

Dear .... , }– greeting

.... }– subject of your letter

Yours sincerely, }– closing line

.... }– your name and signature

Evaluate

5 Swap letters with your partner. Is your partner's letter convincing? Do you think the mayor will come? Why or why not?

6 Tell your partner one thing he or she did really well and one thing he or she might do differently next time.

Editor's checklist

When you finish your work, check it carefully.

- Did you write a draft first?
- Did you include two different addresses?
- Did you include a subject?
- Did you write a salutation?
- Did you give reasons and explanations?
- Did you check your spelling and grammar?

Project 22

Speaking and listening

1. Have a class debate. As a class choose a topic to discuss:
   - new library opening hours
   - free public transport for students
   - summer art or music camp for primary school students.

   1. Work with a partner to create a list of the arguments for and against.

   2. Decide on your point of view for the debate and prepare your argument.

   3. During the class debate, try to:
      - present your arguments clearly, giving reasons
      - ask questions of the opponents
      - listen carefully for information
      - take notes and jot down your ideas as the debate develops.

Evaluate

4. Take a vote at the end of the debate.

   Which arguments were the most convincing - the arguments for or against the topic?

Word builder

> **Look and learn**
> A **morpheme** is a group of letters that has meaning. For example: *sub, auto, tele, graph*.

1. Match each morpheme to the correct meaning and write them into your notebook.

   For example: *sub = under*

auto	small
graph	write
micro	again
mobile	move
vision	see
re	distance
scope	self
tele	see

2. Work with a partner. Choose a morpheme from the list above. Create a list of words that contain the morpheme you have chosen. For example: *sub – submarine, subdivide, subtract, subheading, submit*. Use a dictionary for help if you need it, but make sure you know the meanings of the words you add to your list.

3. Choose three words from your list in Activity 2. Draw a picture to show each word. Try to show the meaning of the morpheme in your drawing.

Project 22 – Parish councils in the news

Let's read

1. Discuss the following questions as a class:

   1. Do you ever read the news? How do you do this (for example online, a newspaper)?

   2. Do you ever watch the news on television?

   3. What sort of information might you miss out on if you never find out the news? Does it matter?

2. As a class, search online for a local newspaper article. Read the newspaper headline and answer the questions before you read the article.

   1. In which newspaper did this article appear?

   2. On which date was the article published?

   3. Who wrote the article?

   4. Can you predict from the headline what the article is about?

3. Read the article silently by yourself. Think about how you can summarise what the article is about.

4. Work with a partner. Discuss the newspaper article and take turns describing what the article is about.

5. Make a summary of the report in your notebook. Be sure to include who or what the article is about along with any other important details.

6 Discuss the following questions with a partner:
- Do you think this article is helpful to readers?
- Does the article include a photograph?
- What purpose does the photograph serve?
- Is the article addressing a problem?
- What do you think the purpose of the article is?

Project 22 – Parish councils in the news

Grammar builder

Remember ⭐☆☆

When we write, we can link ideas and sentences with words such as *because, and, so, as a result, as well as*.

Look and learn

We can also use linking words that help to show a **sequence of events**. For example:

also, first, then, after that.

1. The passage below is about a Town Hall meeting. Work in pairs to choose linking words from the box to show the sequence of events at the meeting.

> We had a Town Hall meeting yesterday to talk about the issues our community is facing. ¹_____ the mayor greeted the community members. ²_____ he introduced the councillors for the communities in the constituency. ³_____ the mayor went through the agenda, so that people would know the topics for discussion. There were several problems. ⁴_____, the roads needed to be repaired, because the pot holes were making it difficult for persons to get to school and work. ⁵_____, a number of the street lights needed to be replaced after being damaged in the last hurricane years ago. One community member suggested using solar-powered lights. ⁶_____, the Community Centre needed to be refurbished. Community members said that they raised more than half the money but would need a pledge from the parish council for the rest so that they could begin the project. ⁷_____, it was suggested that a large reserve water tank should be installed at the home for the aged so that they had a steady water supply when there are water lock offs in the area.
> ⁸_____ the people from the community were sharing their concerns, the mayor and the councillors listened and made notes. ⁹_____, the mayor thanked the people for coming to the Town Hall meeting and promised to work toward fixing the problems.

| secondly | after that | first | then | firstly |
| at the end | while | thirdly | lastly | |

2. Check your work before you finish. Have you used all the linking words? Are you happy they are in the correct places?

   1. Swap with another pair to check and compare your work.

   2. If you were writing the report yourself, would you use the same linking words or can you think of any others you could use instead? Why would yours be better?

Let's write

Task

You are going to write a news report about a problem in the parish where you live and how the parish council is trying to solve the problem.

ICT opportunity

Most newspapers these days are available online and they are easy to read online.

Plan

1. Work in groups. Each person in the group should read different newspapers and look for reports about problems in your parish. Use a diagram to make notes about what you read. Report back to your group with the key ideas:
   - What is the problem?
   - What is being done to solve the problem?
   - What will happen if the problem is not solved?
   - What other suggestions can you think of for how to solve the problem?

2. Work alone. Decide which problem you will write about and do some further research on the problem.

Write

3. Draft your report, like this:

   Paragraph 1: Write a short summary of your whole report.

   Paragraph 2: Give the name of the parish and explain what the problem is. Explain what will happen if the problem continues.

   Paragraph 3: Explain what the parish council is doing about the problem. You can also mention what ordinary people in the parish are doing to help solve the problem.

   Paragraph 4: Say why it will or will not work. Add other ideas you have to help solve the problem and why you think they might work.

4. Think of an interesting headline for your report.

Project 22 – Parish councils in the news

Look and learn

- Headlines should be short and they should attract the reader's attention. Choose your words carefully.
- Using words that start with the same letter can be quite effective, for example:

> **Portland pushes for change**

> **Saint Ann says NO to crime**

Evaluate

5. Edit and improve your report using the "Editor's checklist". Then swap with your partner to read each other's work.

Editor's checklist

When you finish your work, check it carefully.

- Did you include an interesting headline?
- Did you include a short summary paragraph?
- Did you research the facts before you started writing?
- Did you explain what the problem is and how it is being solved?
- Did you say whether you think the solution will work?
- Did you check your spelling and grammar?

Project 23

 **Speaking and listening**

> **VISITORS SHALL NOT CUT OR PICK ANY FLOWER, LEAF OR TWIG, NOT IN ANY WAY INJURE ANY PLANT.**

1. Your teacher will read you some extracts from The Parish Councils Act. The extracts are about the Public Gardens in Spanish Town and the Old Harbour. These by-laws were drawn up more than a hundred years ago. Some of them are still useful, but there are other laws that could be added. For example, there are no laws about dogs or motor vehicles.

   - Should people be allowed to cycle or skateboard?
   - What about playing music?
   - What about safety?

Project 23 – Rules and regulations

2 Work in groups. Discuss how you could update the Spanish Town and Old Harbour By-laws.

- Are there any old by-laws that you would change?
- Are there any new ones that you would add?

3 After everyone has spoken, discuss the pros and cons of some of the by-laws that have been suggested. Would they work well? Why or why not?

4 Write your new list of by-laws or park rules on a poster and present them to your class for discussion. Use a diagram on your poster to show the pros and cons of the suggested by-laws.

Remember ☆☆☆

You must allow other people to state their opinions. You may not agree with them, but you must respect their right to speak.

- Be polite when you are discussing other people's ideas and give reasons why you agree and disagree.
- Take turns speaking.

Word builder

Vocabulary box

border	exhibited	observe	prosecuted
by-law	expose	offence	safety
contravene	handbill	placard	strictly
disorderly	injure	prohibited	

e	x	h	i	b	i	t	e	d	e
o	h	a	l	o	n	r	f	i	x
f	i	n	l	r	j	i	a	s	p
f	b	d	b	d	u	c	s	o	o
e	o	b	s	e	r	v	e	r	s
n	t	i	h	r	e	j	u	d	e
c	p	l	a	c	a	r	d	e	p
e	t	l	d	r	e	b	o	r	l
o	e	s	t	r	i	c	t	l	y
r	d	h	s	a	f	e	t	y	c

1. Which words from the vocabulary box can you find in this wordsearch? Write the words neatly in your notebook and learn to spell them.
2. Find the four words that are not in the wordsearch.
3. Some words have more than one meaning. We often need to use the context of the sentence to determine the meaning.

> address   date   safe   break

1. Look up the meanings of the words above in a dictionary.
2. Write a sentence containing each word for each of its meanings.
3. Work with a partner. How many other words can you think of that have more than one meaning?

Project 23 – Rules and regulations

Let's read

Look and learn

To make a summary, you need to find the main ideas in a text:
- Underline or highlight key words.
- Then, using your own words, rewrite the main ideas in short, simple sentences.

For example:

Sentence in report	Summary
Last night, at about 6 p.m., a young child was attacked by a dog in Green Park.	A dog bit a child in Green Park last night.

Dog attacks child

16 June

Last night, at about 6 p.m., a young child was attacked by a dog in Green Park.

"We were walking in the park. This big dog came running towards my child. My child was afraid, so he started to run away," said the child's mother. "The dog's owner did nothing!"

The dog attacked the boy and bit him on the arm. As a result, the boy had to have medical treatment at the hospital.

The parents of the boy are very upset about this. "It isn't safe in the park anymore. The dog's owner didn't obey the park rules," cried the mother. "I'm going to write to the mayor and the police about this. Someone must enforce the rules. Our children's safety is important!"

1. Read the newspaper report. Then make a summary of the report in your own words.
2. Work in pairs. Can you guess from the article what rules Green Park might have that were broken?
3. Write a new rule for Green Park.

Grammar builder

> ### Look and learn
>
> - When we speak, we often shorten words by leaving letters out. We call these **contractions**. When we write, we use an apostrophe to show that we have left out a letter.
>
>   For example: *I **don't** like that rule. (**Don't** is short for **do not**.)*
>
> - We can also use an apostrophe to show that something **belongs** to someone.
>
>   For example: *It is Susan**'s** dog.*
>
> - Read this sentence from the newspaper report and find the apostrophes.
>
>   *The **dog's** owner **didn't** obey the park rules.*
>
>   **dog's:** shows possession, that the dog belongs to someone
>
>   **didn't:** is a contraction of *did not*

1 Read the newspaper report in "Let's read" lesson again. Find all the words with apostrophes in the report.

2 Write each word and then write a short explanation to say why there is an apostrophe.

3 Rewrite the following sentences correctly, inserting apostrophes where they are necessary.

   1 Is that Sherwins skateboard on the road?

   2 "Im going to the park to play", said Peter.

   3 "Its raining at the moment. Ill come when the rain stops," replied Talia.

   4 We visited the mayors office yesterday.

   5 She didnt know that Pauls mom was very ill.

   6 I cant remember when last I saw the neighbours dog.

4 Rewrite the following sentences. Use contractions with apostrophes instead of the bold words.

   1 **She is** playing with her friends in the park.

   2 **They are** reading the rules on the noticeboard.

   3 **We will** write to the mayor about the litter problem in our town.

   4 I **do not** know where the new skate park is.

Project 23 – Rules and regulations

Let's write

Task

Imagine you are the parents of the child in the newspaper article. You are going to write a letter or an email to the mayor.

Plan

1   Draft your letter considering:
   - your experience of the park
   - what you think should be done to make the park safe
   - what style your letter or email should be written in
   - vocabulary you could use.

Write

2   Type or write your letter, setting it out correctly.

Editor's checklist

When you finish your work, check it carefully.

- Have you written in a style that is suitable for the task?
- Have you explained why as well as what?
- Have you used your new vocabulary?
- Have you used connecting words?

Project 24

 **Speaking and listening**

Today you are going to discuss rules, regulations and tips for speaking and listening.

1 As a class, discuss situations when you need to use speaking and listening skills (for example, talking to friends, talking to adults, giving a presentation, during a debate or in class). Create a list.

2 Work with a partner to discuss speaking and listening skills. Consider:
- What makes a good listener?
- What makes a good speaker?
- Does it depend on the situation? Some examples are giving a presentation, during a debate, during class or talking with friends.

3 Make a list of good speaking and listening skills. Try to include some examples.

4 In small groups, create a poster or presentation about good speaking and listening skills to present to the class.

Project 24 – Local governments in other Caribbean countries

Word builder

Vocabulary box

administrator	district	maintenance	president
affect	elected	manager	prime minister
appoint	laws	municipal	quarter
chairperson	local	corporation	service
chief executive officer (CEO)		national	vote

1. Work in pairs. Read each word from the vocabulary box aloud in random order. Let your partner find each word as you read. Look up the meanings of words that you do not know.

2. Read the vocabulary box and find these words:
   - six nouns that could describe leaders in any government
   - two areas into which a country or place can be divided.

   Then compare your lists with your partner's list.

Remember ☆☆☆

A **noun** is the name of a person, place or thing.

Look and learn

We can divide words up into the sounds they make using our knowledge of diagraphs and trigraphs. For example:

c	l	er	k

This helps us to read and pronounce words.

215

3 1 Put these words into sound boxes. Draw the boxes in your notebook and fill in the sounds.

street

parish

breach

chief

market

park

2 Choose four words from the vocabulary box and put them into sound boxes in your notebook.

Project 24 – Local governments in other Caribbean countries

Let's read

1. Before you read, work in groups and make a list of all the types of work people who serve in local governments should do.

    - Think about parish councils.
    - If you have been to other countries in the Caribbean, think about what you have seen there, too.

Local governments

Countries usually have a national government as well as a local government. The national government is responsible for things that affect the whole country. The leader of a national government is usually a president or a prime minister.

Most countries are divided into smaller areas. Each area has its own local government, which deals with things that affect these local communities. These are called *parishes*, *councils*, *quarters* or *districts*.

Countries in the Caribbean have different systems of local government. In some countries, such as Jamaica, people vote for some of the people who serve in their local government. In other countries, such as Barbados and Saint Lucia for example, people do not vote for their local councillors. Councillors are appointed by the national government.

2. Work with a partner. Read the table on the next page carefully. Ask each other questions to compare the local governments of Jamaica and Trinidad and Tobago. Here are some questions you can use:

    1. Are the councillors elected or appointed in _____?
    2. Which country has municipal corporations?
    3. How are the leaders of local government in _____ called?
    4. How many _____ are there in _____?
    5. What are the responsibilities of the local government in _____?

	Jamaica	Trinidad and Tobago
Type of local government	parish councils	municipal corporations
Number of areas	12 parishes + Portmore Municipal Council and KSAC (Kingston and St Andrew Corporation)	Trinidad has 14 counties run by municipal corporations; Tobago has a House of Assembly
Leaders	mayors and managers	mayors and chairpersons, chief executive officers
Elected or appointed	elected councillors, appointed administrators	elected councillors, appointed administrators
Responsibilities	water supplies, markets, waste removal, street lighting, some road maintenance, public land, animal management, passing and implementing local laws	water supplies, markets, waste removal, street lighting, some road maintenance, public land, animal management, passing and implementing local laws

3. Compare local governments. Discuss the following questions with your partner:
   - What do Jamaica and Trinidad and Tobago do in the same way?
   - What do these countries do differently and why?
   - Do you think you would notice the difference if you visited Trinidad and Tobago?

Research and study skills

Choose a Caribbean country and find out the following about the local government in that country:

- type of government
- number of areas
- leaders
- responsibilities.

ICT opportunity

You can find this information online on government websites. Type "local government" and the name of the country into your search engine.

Project 24 – Local governments in other Caribbean countries

Grammar builder

Remember ☆☆☆

Punctuation helps us to read and understand a text.

The essentials: • capital letters • full stops • question marks	Very useful: • commas • semi-colons	More: • exclamation marks
We cannot write a sentence without these marks.	These show us where to pause and that parts of a sentence are connected.	These help us to add feeling or expression to a sentence.

1 Rewrite the following paragraphs with punctuation and capital letters to make them easier to read.

   1 jamaica is divided up into smaller areas called *parishes* which are run by councils trinidad and tobago on the other hand has counties which are run by local municipal corporations Tobago has a house of assembly

   2 our parish councils have to make sure that we all have access to water and that our garbage is removed the council also makes sure that roads are repaired and that people obey the rules of the road if there is a disaster such as a hurricane they help people

2 Compare your punctuation in Activity 1 with your partner's.

- Is the punctuation the same?
- Whose do you think is clearer?
- Explain what you have done differently and why.

3 Edit and improve your paragraphs after your discussion.

219

Term 2 Unit 2

Let's write

Task

You are going to write two paragraphs about the local government of another Caribbean country.

Plan

1. Do some research. Decide on two main ideas that you want to write about.

ICT opportunity

Do some research on the internet. Remember that not everything we read on the internet is accurate, so look at a few different websites to compare the information. The government of a country usually has the most accurate information about the country.

2. Plan your paragraphs using the diagram below. You could use subheadings.

How local government is organised.

The responsibilities of local government.

Write

3. Draft your paragraphs. Start with your topic sentence and write another two to three sentences for each paragraph.

220

Project 24 – Local governments in other Caribbean countries

Editor's checklist

Look out for the following when checking your partner's work:

- Has your partner used the correct vocabulary? For example, is the country divided into "parishes" or "districts"?
- Does each paragraph have a topic sentence? Does it introduce the paragraph well?
- Is each paragraph clear and easy to understand?
- Are there any spelling mistakes? Can you correct them?

4 Write your final paragraphs neatly on a sheet of paper and display it in the class for others to read.

It is always good to know how things work in other countries!

Evaluate

5 Work with a partner. Check each other's paragraphs.

- Discuss them and give some useful advice about how to improve the work.
- Read the notes in the "Editor's checklist".

Term 2 Unit 2 Review and assessment

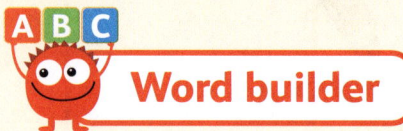
Word builder

1. There are five spelling mistakes in the sentences below. Rewrite the sentences correctly in your notebook.

   > Mrs Brown is the mayer of Kingston, which is the capitol citee of Jamaica. Mr Cumberbatch is the chairpersun of a parish counsil.

2. The mayor is making a speech. Choose synonyms from the box below to replace the bold words in the speech.

   > prosperous   commerce   contravene   launching   prohibited

   > Greetings to you all!
   >
   > Let's make our parish a place that we are all proud of! We are going to make sure that people do not **break** the laws of our parish. Disorderly behaviour will **not** be **allowed**.
   >
   > I am **starting** a campaign to clean up the parish. Let's make our parish **rich** and successful.
   >
   > Let's develop **trade** in the parish.

Review and assessment

 **Let's read**

1 Read the text about the parish of Westmoreland. Then complete the summary table.

> Westmoreland Parish is on the south-western part of Jamaica. The parish of Hanover is to the north and the parishes of St James and St Elizabeth are to the east. The capital is Savanna-la-Mar. Negril is an important tourist destination in the parish. Several rivers run through this fertile parish, including the Cabritta, the Negril, the New Savanna and Morgan's. Crops such as sugar cane, bananas, coffee and ginger are grown. Fishing and cattle-raising are also important commercial activities.

Parish:	
Capital city:	
Other important towns:	
Rivers:	
Commerce:	

G Grammar builder

1 Rewrite this passage with the correct punctuation and capital letters.

> st james parish is one of jamaica's smallest parishes. its on the north-western part of jamaica. the capital and main port is montego bay. the nassau mountains stretch across the parish.

223

2 Use the best connecting words to combine the following sentences.

| We are eager for the end of the day | since | summer holiday begins tomorrow! |

| Our parents have plans to go to the beach this weekend | because | something comes up at work. |

| After that we intend to watch movies for a whole week | but | we are not allowed to watch TV during the school term. |

| Our cousin from the USA wants to visit Jamaica this summer | when | her parents are thinking of sending her to a music camp. |

| I know that we will be very happy to see our friends again | unless | we return to school after the summer. |

Let's write

- Write about a problem in your parish. You can either write a newspaper report or you can write a letter to the mayor of the parish. In your report or letter:
    - explain clearly what the problem is
    - give facts (dates and names of places)
    - suggest a solution to the problem.

- In your writing, demonstrate that you:
    - know the correct format for a letter or a report
    - can give factual information
    - can use correction punctuation and spelling
    - can check and edit your work.

Unit 1

Project 25

Speaking and listening

1. Look at the photographs carefully. For each photograph, discuss with your partner or group:
   - what you see in the photograph
   - how you feel about the photograph.

Look and learn

To make **questions**, use question words such as *When, How, Why, Where, What*.

For example: *What type of pollution is a problem in this parish? Where does the pollution come from?*

You can also start with words like *Do, Does, Is, Are, Have*.

For example: *Have you seen any smoke in the air this month? Do you sneeze and cough all the time because of pollution?*

2. Work with a partner. Think of five questions to ask about the photographs. Use the following openers:
   - Where …?
   - Why …?
   - When …?
   - What …?
   - How …?

Word builder

Vocabulary box

pollution	factory	poisonous	land
die	breathe	unhealthy	water
oil	sick	polluted	kill
smoke	rubbish/trash	air	

1 Read all the words in the vocabulary box carefully. Write down the words that you do not know and find out what they mean.

2 Read the following captions and copy them in your notebook. Underline all the words from the vocabulary box. Then match the captions to the photographs on page 225.

   1 Water is polluted by rubbish or by oil leaking from big ships. This can kill the animals that live in the water.

   2 Smoke from factories, cars and ships pollutes the air. People and animals who live nearby get sick when they breathe in this air; plants may also die.

   3 The land becomes unhealthy and polluted when people leave their trash lying around or when they let poisonous substances run into the ground or water.

Remember ☆☆☆

A **synonym** is a word that has a similar meaning to another word. For example, some synonyms for the word *big* are: *huge, large, massive, gigantic, enormous*.

We can use synonyms to make our writing sound more interesting and vary our vocabulary; a **thesaurus** lists synonyms.

3 Use a thesaurus to find synonyms for each of the following words: *sick, trash, pollution, unhealthy*.

Let's read

1. Look at the poem *Dreamer* again. Are you a dreamer? What do you dream about? Discuss this with the class.

2. Listen as your teacher reads this poem to you.

Dreamer

I dreamt I was an ocean
and no one polluted me.

I dreamt I was a whale
and no hunters chased after me.

I dreamt I was the air
and nothing blackened me.

I dreamt I was a stream
and nobody poisoned me.

I dreamt I was an elephant
and nobody stole my ivory.

I dreamt was a rain forest
and no one cut down my trees.

I dreamt I painted a smile
on the face of the Earth
for all to see.

by Brian Moses

---

3. Discuss and answer the following questions.

   1. Who is the dreamer in this poem?

   2. What does this person dream about?

   3. Why does the dreamer want to paint a smile on the face of the Earth?

   4. How did you feel when you listened to this poem?

4. Work in groups. Convert the poem into Jamaican Creole (JC).

> **Remember** ☆☆☆
>
> **Personification** is when writers give objects/things human qualities or characteristics. For example:
> *The branches of the tree waved at me.*

5 Work with a partner. Reread the poem. Can you find any examples of personification?

6 1 Find all of the examples from the poem of ways that humans harm living things and the Earth. Make a list of them in your notebook.

   2 Discuss each problem on your list with a partner. What do you know about this problem? How is it caused by humans?

   3 Share your ideas with the class.

Research and study skills

1 Search the internet to find poems or songs about pollution. Choose your favourite poem and read it to your partner.

2 Type the poem or write it in your best handwriting and decorate it with pictures. Display the poem in your classroom.

> **What's your view?**
> Are there different kinds of dreams? What kind of dream is the poet writing about?

Grammar builder

Remember ☆ ☆ ☆

- We usually add -d or -ed to verbs to make the past simple. For example:

  Yesterday we played a game.

  The smoke from the ship polluted the air.

- Some verbs are **irregular** and change completely in the past simple. For example:

  We went to see the factory last week.

  We put gas in the car yesterday.

- Here are some other irregular verbs. Do you know them?

  cut   buy   come   do   eat   get   give   throw   make   have   leave   win

1 Read the poem *Dreamer* on page 228 again. Find all the verbs that are in the past simple and write them down.

2 Make a sentence with each verb in another verb tense that you know. For example: *The cat is chasing a mouse* (present continuous).

3 Write these sentences in the past simple.

   1 The factory pollutes the nearby town.

   2 We cough and sneeze when we breathe in the polluted air.

   3 They cut down all the trees to plant crops.

   4 Sally leaves all her trash on the table!

   5 Tyrone throws all his trash in the trash can.

   6 The birds die because of the oil in the water.

   7 Some people make a mess when they have a picnic.

   8 Sarah wins the competition!

Project 25 – Pollution

Let's write

L👀k and learn

Similes

A simile is a phrase that compares a person, place or thing to something else. For example:

*The water was **as** clear **as** glass.*

*The rubbish bin was yellow **like** a buttercup.*

Metaphors

A metaphor is a phrase that describes a person, place or thing as something else. For example:

The ocean was a rubbish dump.

Onomatopoeia

Onomatopoeic are the words that sound like the word they are describing.
For example: *buzz, crash, bang, whizz, pop.*

The waves crashed on the sand.

Personification

Personification is when a person, place or thing is given human qualities or characteristics.

For example: *The bin gobbled the rubbish.*

The black oil swallowed the ocean.

The trash choked the ocean.

1. Work in pairs. You are going to write your own poem or song about pollution. You can write the poem in Standard Jamaican English (SJE) or in Jamaican Creole (JC). Can you include similes, metaphors, onomatopoeia or personification?

   *You could use the same format as the poem **Dreamer** or you could write a rhyming poem.*

Remember ☆☆☆

When writing a short story, poem or a long essay, remember these key processes:

- brainstorm your ideas
- draft
- edit and improve

Term 3 Unit 1

Project 26

Speaking and listening

1   First look at this headline from *The Gleaner, 5 February 2017* and then discuss the following questions as a class.

> **Pollution crisis – Portmore residents with respiratory illnesses urged to flee foul community**

   1   What is the problem in Portmore?

   2   Who is affected by the problem?

   3   Why do you think they have this problem in Portmore?

2   Now read this quote from the Jamaican Environment Trust (JET) organisation: "The main sources of air pollution in Jamaica are industrial, motor vehicle emissions, open burning by individuals and businesses, garbage dumps, and forest or bushfires." Discuss the questions with a partner.

   1   What causes air pollution in Jamaica?

   2   Can you suggest any other causes of air pollution?

3   Now look at the photographs and think about your own community. As a class, discuss what types of air pollution exist in your parish.

Project 26 – Collecting information

> Write down your ideas on a mind map. You will use the ideas later on in this project.

> Remember to respect other people's opinions even when they are different to your own.

4 Work in groups. You are going to carry out a survey to find out more about air pollution in your parish.

1. Make up a list of six questions to ask. Use the following openers:
   - Who …?
   - Where …?
   - Why …?
   - When …?
   - What …?

2. Select ten different people and ask each person the same six questions.

3. Record your answers very carefully.

233

Word builder

Vocabulary box

emissions	dumps	foul	fumes
sources	bushfires	acid rain	chemical
industrial	crisis	pollutants	destroy
burning	respiratory	gas	

1. Read all the words in the vocabulary box aloud with your partner.

2. Work out the meaning of the underlined words in the following sentences. Look at the whole sentence for clues about the meaning.

   1. People who already have <u>respiratory</u> diseases, such as asthma, find that pollution makes their breathing difficulties worse.

   2. Pollutants can be gas <u>emissions</u>, such as carbon monoxide, which come from vehicles and factories.

   3. The rain kills trees and other plants because it burns the leaves of plants and <u>destroys</u> them.

3. The following words are all part of the same word family: *pollute, polluted, pollutant, polluter, pollution*. Look up each word in your dictionary.

   1. What part of speech is it – a noun, a verb or an adjective?

   2. Make a sentence to show that you understand the meaning of each word.

4. Choose six words from the vocabulary box that have more than one syllable.

   1. Write the words in alphabetical order in your notebook.

   2. Practise spelling each word with a partner until you feel confident.

Remember ☆☆☆

Remember to break long words into syllables. This makes them easier to read.

Let's read

1. Skim this text quickly and tell your partner what you think it is about.
2. Read the text with your partner until you think you understand the main ideas.

Remember ☆☆☆

Always read the headings and subheadings and look at the photographs. Read the captions under the photographs.

How does air pollution affect plants and animals?

Pollution can make the air dirty. The things that pollute the air are called *air pollutants*. They reach the air by natural processes or through human activities. Pollutants spread easily through the air and affect plants and animals that breathe in the air. Pollutants can cause respiratory illnesses. People who already have respiratory diseases such as asthma find that pollution makes their breathing difficulties worse.

Types of air pollution

Pollutants can be gas emissions, such as carbon monoxide gas that comes from vehicles and factories. Vehicles and factories also give off fumes, which are another type of air pollution. When we burn garbage, small particles go up into the air. These particles also pollute the air.

Acid rain

Air pollutants enter the air and mix with other gases. The pollutants mix with droplets of water and make the water droplets acidic. When this acid rain falls, it is very harmful to plants. The rain kills trees and other plants because it burns the leaves and destroys them. Plants cannot breathe and make crops if they have no leaves, so they die. Acid rain also harms the animals, fish and other wildlife.

Animals need plants to survive

Animals need plants for food and shelter. If air pollution damages these plants, animals have less food to eat and fewer places to live.

Bibliography

www.eschooltoday.com
www.windows2universe.org
Maciver, Angus: *Illustrated First Aid in English*, 2015, London, Hodder Education
Morrissey, Mike: *Caribbean School Atlas Skills Workbook*, 2015, London, Hodder Education

This is what acid rain does to a forest.

3 Make notes about the main ideas in the text you have read.

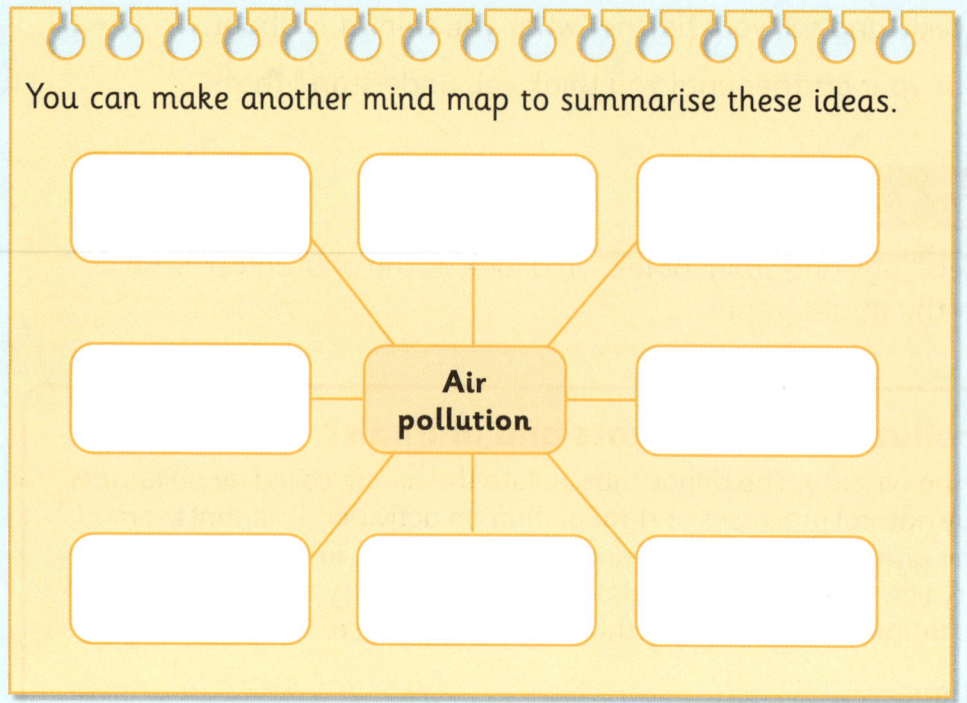

4 Look at the text again and answer the questions.

1. Is this a fiction text, or a non-fiction text? Use a diagram such as a table or a Venn diagram to explain the difference.

2. What is a bibliography? Why might some texts include a bibliography?

3. What do you think the purpose of this text is?

5 Imagine that you have been asked to share the information from this text with a group of Grade 2 students. Think about:

- How you would present the information, such as a presentation or a poster
- What information you would include, and how you would explain it
- Any information or vocabulary that you might not include, and why.

Grammar builder

> **Look and learn**
>
> **Collective nouns** are groups of people, places or things.
> For example: *a crowd of people, a herd of cows, a class of pupils.*

1. Copy the sentences in your notebook. Underline the collective noun.

   1. The pollution posters were created by the class of pupils.
   2. We presented the mayor with a bouquet of flowers.
   3. I spotted a fleet of ships through the binoculars.
   4. There was a hive of bees in the garden.
   5. A crowd of people had gathered outside the town hall.
   6. In the field, was a herd of cows.

2. Work with a partner. How many collective nouns can you think of? Research collective nouns; look in the dictionary and search on the internet.

3. Work with a partner to create a list of collective nouns.

4. Create a poster about collective nouns to display in your classroom.

Let's write

1. Work in groups and draw up a checklist for evaluating reports. Look at the report you read on page 235 again. What do you need to include? What sort of language should you use?

2. Work in pairs. You are going to write a short report about air pollution in your parish. You can use the mind map you have compiled as well as the data from the survey you conducted. Your report should be about 200 words long. You need to include a short bibliography in your report to say where you found your information.

Look and learn

A **bibliography** is a list of the books or articles that you used when you collected the information for this project. Write the names of the books like this, in alphabetical order according to the surname of the author: *Brown, James Dudley: Is Acid Rain a problem? Kingston Press, Jamaica 2017*. Write the name of the publisher and the year in which it was published, too. If you used websites, write the names of the websites like this: www.eschooltoday.com

ICT opportunity

You can do your research online by simply typing in the words "air pollution" in the search engine on your computer.

Evaluate

3. Then use the checklist your group drew up to evaluate your own report. What do you think you did well? Did you forget anything? What can you improve?

Project 27

Speaking and listening

1 Read what some people have to say about air pollution.

- How do we stop air pollution?
- Care about the air you breathe!
- What's the solution?
- So much smoke in the sky!
- Don't get sick – take action!
- Just makes me want to cry.
- Why, oh, why?
- We need cars and factories! Don't fuss about pollution.
- Breathing has become dangerous to our health!

2 Do you agree or disagree with these statements? Why?
3 Which statement do you think you will remember? Why?

Look and learn

A **slogan** is a short phrase that you can easily remember. Slogans are often used in advertisements to help people remember a product. "Go green to breathe clean" is a slogan.

Remember to respect other people's opinions even when they are different to your own.

4 As a class, discuss and create a list of all different ways to reduce and tackle air pollution.

5 Work in small groups. Role play different scenes that show ways of reducing and tackling air pollution.

Project 27 – Protest against pollution

Word builder

Vocabulary box

solution	billow	compost	control
breathe	handkerchief	recycling	protest
slogan	truck	coughed	heap
cloud	collect	continued	dirty

1 The letters in the following words from the vocabulary box are jumbled. Write them correctly.

> ganslo   wollib   kerchiefhand   postcom
> tolcont   testpro   eathbre   ouldc   tiosolun

2 Look at the photographs. Work out what the underlined words in the captions mean.

Remember ☆☆☆

Look for clues in the photographs and in the words in the captions.

Smoke <u>billows</u> from a factory chimney.

A <u>heap</u> of rubbish in the countryside.

<u>Recycling</u> reduces the amount of garbage we throw away.

Smoke causes <u>coughing</u> and other health problems.

241

3 Find words in the vocabulary box to complete these expressions:

1 a _____ of rubbish
2 a _____ of smoke
3 to _____ the garbage
4 to _____ bushfires
5 to _____ clean air
6 _____ plastic helps the environment

Project 27 – Protest against pollution

Let's read

1. Skim the newspaper article below. Which problem does it raise?

> ### Burning garbage
>
> Yesterday, I was walking down the street on my way to the port. First I smelled it – then I saw it. Great clouds of black smoke billowing up into the air.
>
> "What's going on?" I asked someone.
>
> "Oh, people are burning their garbage," said a passer-by who was walking with a handkerchief over his face.
>
> "Don't they know that it's bad for our health?" I asked.
>
> "Maybe," said the man. "But what do you do with the garbage? The trucks don't come here to collect it," said the man.
>
> "What about compost heaps and recycling?" I asked.
>
> "Who has time for that?" said the man.
>
> I coughed and continued my walk. I don't want to breathe in all this pollution, I thought to myself. How do we solve this problem? And what happens if the fires get out of control? Who puts them out? It's time to protest about this! As our mayor says: "Time for action!"

2. Read the article with a partner. Make a summary of the main ideas in this article. Start like this:

   This article is about the problem of ….
   People … because … This causes ….

3. Answer the questions and complete the following tasks.

   1. What is the problem in the article?

   2. What solutions are suggested?

   3. Work in small groups. Role play the scene from the newspaper article.

4. Imagine that you are walking down a street. You see people burning garbage. Write down:

   - two questions that you would ask them
   - two comments that you could make
   - two pieces of advice you would give people about this.

Grammar builder

> **Look and learn**
>
> Use **quotation marks** ("") when you write to show what people say.
> For example: *"What about compost heaps and recycling?" I asked.*
> Remember that the quotation marks go at the beginning and the end of the words. The other punctuation marks go inside the quotation marks.

1. Reread the newspaper article *Burning garbage*. Show your partner where the quotation marks are used.

2. Discuss with a partner:
   - Why do we use quotation marks in our writing?
   - How do we use quotation marks in our writing?

3. Create a poster to explain how and when to use quotation marks in your writing. Try to include examples. Display your poster in the classroom.

4. Copy these statements in your notebook and add quotation marks where necessary.

   1. We must stop burning our garbage, said Dad.
   2. Smoke is unhealthy. It makes me cough! said Tyrone.
   3. Heaps of garbage are smelly and unhealthy, said the Mayor.
   4. Look at those clouds of smoke from the garbage heaps! said Betty.
   5. Why do people burn their garbage? I asked.

Project 27 – Protest against pollution

Let's write

1. Work in groups. You are going to make a poster about air pollution. The aim of the poster is to make people at your school aware of air pollution. On the poster you should say:

   - why air pollution is harmful
   - what causes air pollution
   - what your community can do about air pollution.

   Your poster should also have a slogan, as well as a quote from a community leader.

   Tips about posters:
   - Remember that people look at posters from a distance, so you need to use big, bold words.
   - Use bright strong colours.
   - You don't need to use full sentences.
   - Choose words that have an impact!

Use a diagram to show causes and effects of pollution, as well as solutions in a clear and simple way.

Editor's checklist

Check your work carefully when you finish.
- Did you use quotation marks for quotes?
- Did you check your spelling?

Project 28

Speaking and listening

> **Look and learn**
> In a **debate**, people argue for and against an idea. They try to convince the people who are listening about something. People listen and then vote for the speakers who are the most convincing. The speakers with the most votes win the debate.

1. You are going to have a class debate about the following subject:

   We cannot have progress without pollution.

   Your teacher will help you to organise this. Some people in the class will need to argue that this statement is true and some people will need to argue that the statement is false. The photographs below will help you with your arguments.

Project 28 – Pollution and progress

Word builder

Vocabulary box

air	coal	kiln lime	progress	space
carbon	easier	limit	quicker	craft
dioxide	improve	need	revolution	succeed
cheap	industrial	new	right	worse

1. With your partner, read each word aloud in a random order. Let your partner find each word as you read. Then look up the words that you do not know in a dictionary.

2. Choose three words from the vocabulary box. Put each word into a sentence to say aloud.

Look and learn

Homophones are words that sound the same, but have different meanings and spellings. For example:

their – something that belongs to some people (*The people sold their house.*)

there – a place, where something is (*The house is over there, near the river.*)

We have to remember what the word means when we spell it.

Homonyms are words that sound the same as other words and are also spelled the same. For example:

die – to stop living

die – small cube that you use to play a game.

3. Match the homophones. Then write them in your notebook and write a sentence for each.

road	son
weight	rain
sun	wait
whale	male
two	rode
mail	too
reign	wail

247

4 Copy the sentences into your notebook. Then fill in the missing homophones.

1. We _____ the horses on the beach. (rode / road / rowed)
2. The _____ was shining brightly all day. (son / sun)
3. I had to _____ 40 minutes for the bus to come. (wait / weight)
4. I sheltered from the _____, at my friend's house. (rain / reign)
5. I have _____ brothers and a sister. (too / two / to)

5 Work with a partner to create a crossword puzzle for the following homophones:

> son   sun   male   mail   wail   whale   road   rowed

6 Work with a partner. Research homophones on the internet and create a list of homophones you find.

7 Write sentences to show each meaning of the following homonyms:

> can   bank   iron   duck   park   saw   well

Let's read

1 Look at the photographs and read the text and captions. What do space crafts have to do with air pollution? Share your ideas.

Has progress caused air pollution?

Air pollution is not new; it started when people learned to make fires. It got worse when people started to burn coal. In the 1300s, air pollution was very bad in England because people used coal to warm their houses and cook food. Many people died from breathing in so much smoke. The King of England, Edward I, tried to stop people burning coal in their homes and in the kilns where they made lime. He didn't succeed because there was a lot of coal in England and it was cheap!

Air pollution became worse after the industrial revolution. People built lots of new factories and big towns grew up around the factories. Look at how the population of the city of Manchester increased between 1801 and 1841, for example. The machines in the factories needed a lot of power. The people who worked in the factories needed houses. So, there was a greater need for fuel; pollution became worse. People died as their countries developed.

Population of city of Manchester, England

1801	1841
35 000	353 000

A town in England in after the industrial revolution.

The problem continues. We always want to make our lives easier and complete things more quickly, so we buy machines to do our work for us. We also use more chemicals and as a result more air pollutants go up into the air. Tourists fly all over the world in aeroplanes and we are able to send spacecrafts up to other planets.

As we continue to improve our way of living, we need to think carefully about what damage we are doing to the air around us. We need to do the right thing; we need to reduce air pollution.

Scientists say that each time we send a space craft up into the air, more than 28 tonnes of the poisonous carbon dioxide gas goes into the air, too!

2 Now read the title of the text again. Does it make sense? Do you agree or disagree? Share your ideas.

Remember to respect other people's opinions even if they are different to yours.

3 Decide if these statements are true or false. Correct the false statements.
1. Air pollution started in modern times. ____
2. Smoke can kill you if you breathe in too much of it. ____
3. People in England used wood to heat their homes in the 1300s. ____
4. Factories made air pollution worse. ____
5. Progress has caused air pollution. ____
6. Spacecrafts do not cause much air pollution. ____

4 Summarise the main points in the article. Use bullet points to write your ideas and read your summary to a partner.

Research and study skills

Work with a partner. Use the internet, library or newspaper articles to find information and research ways to reduce air pollution.
- What phrases or words could you search for?
- Make notes of your findings.
- Create a bibliography of websites, books and articles you used or read during your research.

Project 28 – Pollution and progress

Grammar builder

Look and learn

We can use semi-colons (;) to connect ideas in sentences. We can use them instead of connecting words such as and, but and or. We can also use them instead of writing separate sentences.

Examples

Air pollution is not new. It started when people learned to make fires.
→ *Air pollution is not new; it started when people learned to make fires.*

We need to do the right thing because we need reduce air pollution.
→ *We need to do the right thing; we need reduce air pollution.*

1. Use semi-colons to connect ideas. Choose a sentence from Column A and a sentence from Column B. Rewrite them as one sentence, with a semi-colon.

Column A	Column B
We started a campaign to clean up the parish.	It's good for the environment.
We smelled it.	Unfortunately they also cause pollution.
There is so much garbage.	Now our parish is successful and clean.
Heaps of garbage are smelly.	There were clouds of smoke billowing up into the air.
Recycling reduces the amount of garbage we throw away.	They are also very unhealthy.
We need cars and factories.	The trucks don't collect it.

2. Write two sentences of you own about air pollution. Use semi-colons in your sentences.

3. Discuss this question in groups: *Why is punctuation important?* Then report back to the class with your ideas.

Give examples of five types of punctuation.

Give an example of how each type of punctuation is used in a sentence or paragraph.

251

Term 3 Unit 1

Let's write

> **L👀k and learn**
> Your **point of view** is your opinion about a fact or idea. You have a right to say what you think. Other people should listen to your point of view.

You are going to write a letter or an email to a friend. In the letter or email you are going to tell your friend about something that you have learned about air pollution in your own parish. You need to explain:

- what the problem in your parish is
- what people do (or don't do) about it
- what your point of view is.

1. Read this extract from a letter that Mary-Lou wrote to her friend and work in groups to discuss pollution problems in your own parish. Make notes of the ideas.

> It's so crazy. My neighbours complain about the smoke from the factory in town, but they still make big fires to burn their rubbish! And they drive a big car that gives off smelly gas.

Evaluate

2. Use some of the notes from Activity 1 to write or type a letter or an email. Then evaluate your writing, using the "Editor's checklist".

Editor's checklist

Check your work carefully when you finish.
- Is the email address correct?
- Did you use an appropriate greeting?

Project 29

Speaking and listening

1. Listen as your teacher reads a poem about pollution by Kathleen Wiley.

2. Make notes as you listen. Write down the main points and key words to help you remember.

3. Work with a partner and discuss:
   - **three** main facts from the poem
   - **two** things you found interesting
   - **one** word to describe how you feel about the poem.

4. Compare the information in this poem with the information in a non-fiction text. Draw a simple diagram to compare the texts as you do this.

5. Then discuss what you would prefer to read – a poem or a non-fiction text? Which text will you remember?

Word builder

Vocabulary box

fuel	decayed	heavily	natural gas
fossil fuel	carbon	electricity	commercial
gasoline	transport	oil	residential
coal	rely		

1. A *fuel* is something that we burn to create heat or energy. Write down the names of four fuels in the vocabulary box.

2. Match words from the list to match these definitions.
   1. to depend on something
   2. something that is part of all living things on Earth
   3. rotten
   4. the movement of people and things from one place to another

3. Look at the dictionary definitions below and then answer the questions.
   - resident (noun): a person who lives somewhere for a long time
   - commerce (noun): a business activity that involves buying and selling things
   - heavy (adjective): something that has a great mass or weight

   1. What do the underlined words in the following sentence mean?

      This is a <u>residential</u> property so it may not be used for <u>commercial</u> purposes.
   2. If a person *resides in* a place, what does he or she do?
   3. What is the opposite of *heavy*?
   4. If you rely *heavily* on something, do you need it a lot or a little?

4. Practise spelling the words in the vocabulary box. Work with a partner. Take turns to read out words while your partner writes them. Help your partner by dividing longer words into syllables.

Project 29 – Burning fossil fuels

> **L👀k and learn**
>
> Make up sentences to help you remember how to spell words. Use the letters in the word. This will help you to remember the letters in the word.
>
> For example:
>
> **F**ill
>
> **U**p
>
> **E**arly
>
> **L**ucy

5 Choose a word from the vocabulary box and create a phrase to help you remember how to spell the word. Share you phrase with the class.

255

Let's read

1. Skim through the article *Fossil fuels* and say what you think it is about.
2. Read the article in pairs. Try to understand the main ideas in each paragraph. Read all the labels on the pie chart carefully.

Fossil fuels

Fuels are materials that we burn. Fossil fuels are materials formed over thousands of years from decayed plants and animals under the ground. Coal, oil, natural gas and gasoline are examples of fossil fuels. We burn fossil fuels in order to cook food, to keep warm, to make our cars move, or to make electricity. So fossil fuels are very useful.

However, burning these fuels also creates a lot of air pollution. Fossil fuels contain carbon and when we burn them we get carbon emissions, which are harmful to people, animals and the environment.

This is not a new problem – but it is a growing problem. People used to get sick because they made fires inside their houses. This caused a lot of smoke in the houses, which was very unhealthy. Now we don't have so much smoke inside our houses, but the air outside is polluted with smoke from vehicles and factories. As our countries have developed, we have burned more fossil fuels and, as a result, the air has become more polluted. People use cars, trucks, ships and aeroplanes to move all over the world. We trade with other countries and the goods that we trade have to be moved to different places. Most forms of transport we use still burn fossil fuels.

We also use fossil fuels to make electricity and we rely very heavily on electricity to make things work in our modern world. We are used to being able to switch on lights and machines in our homes. Factories need electricity to make their machines work, for example.

The pie chart below shows how the world uses fossil fuels.

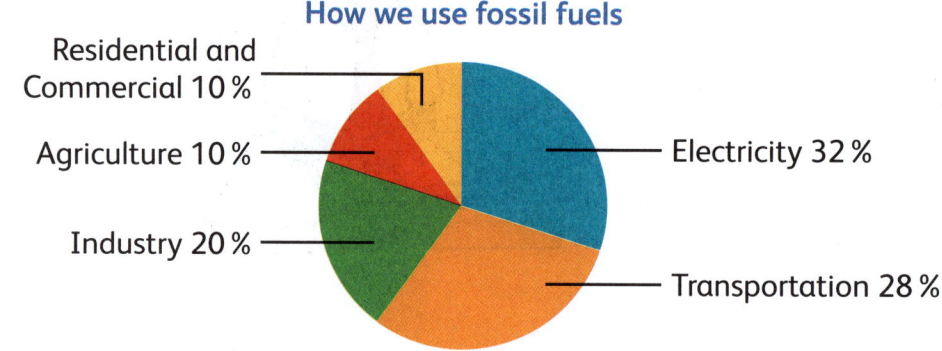

3 Scan the article carefully and decide if the following sentences are true (T) or false (F).

   1 Coal is a fossil fuel. _____
   2 When we burn coal, carbon is given off into the air. _____
   3 Fossil fuels are not useful. _____
   4 Burning fossil fuels causes air pollution. _____
   5 Air pollution is getting worse. _____

4 Answer the following questions according to the text.

   1 Why do we use fossil fuels? Give two uses.
   2 How much fossil fuel is used for "residential and commercial" purposes?
   3 For which things do we use fossil fuels the most?
   4 Why do we use more on fossil fuels than we used to?

5 Draw a diagram to show how fossil fuel turns into air pollution. Include why this is dangerous in your diagram. Write a caption for each part of your diagram to explain what it shows.

ICT opportunity

Use the internet to find the amount of emissions each person in Jamaica creates. Look at the emissions per person in some other countries, too. How does Jamaica compare? Why might this happen?

Term 3 Unit 1

Grammar builder

Look and learn

We use **pronouns** so that we don't have to repeat names in sentences. It sounds better to use a pronoun than to repeat a word in a sentence.

Pronouns can be used as subjects or objects in sentences. Here are some pronouns you should know:

I   you   he   she   it   we   you   they   (**subject pronouns**)
me   you   him   her   it   we   you   them   (**object pronouns**)

We use **possessive pronouns** such as mine, ours, yours, his, hers, theirs to show that something belongs to someone.

Examples:
*Our families both have black cars. This is **ours**. Which is **yours**?*

1. Improve these sentences by replacing the underlined words with pronouns from the box. You can use the pronouns more than once.

    1. Fossil fuels are useful. We burn <u>fossil fuels</u>.
    2. Coal is a fossil fuel. We can burn <u>coal</u>.
    3. This is not their house. <u>Their house</u> doesn't have a chimney.
    4. There is some smoke coming out of the house. Can you see <u>the smoke</u>?
    5. The girl is coughing and sneezing. Can you help <u>the girl</u>?
    6. The man is protesting about air pollution. Let's join <u>the man</u>.

2. Work with a partner. Read these sentences and find the pronouns. Then say what noun each pronoun is replacing (or what noun the pronoun refers to).

    For example:

    Factories need electricity to make their machines work.

    Their refers to the factories.

    1. Fossil fuels contain carbon. Burning them causes carbon emissions.
    2. The air is so polluted today. It is full of smoke!
    3. Mary says that she feels sick. She says she can't breathe well.
    4. The boys are joining in the protest. They want to help stop air pollution.
    5. Is that his bag? It is almost the same as mine.

Project 29 – Burning fossil fuels

Let's write

1. Different types of writing require different styles, features and layouts. Work with a partner to research texts about pollution (you could use the internet, the library or texts in this book).

    1. Find an example of each text:
        - newspaper report
        - story
        - poem
        - information text
        - leaflet or poster
        - letter

    2. With your partner, discuss the similarities and differences between each text type.

    3. Choose two different pieces of writing about the topic "pollution", for example a story and a newspaper report. Compare the two pieces of writing. What is similar and what is different? Draw a Venn diagram in your notebook and fill it in.

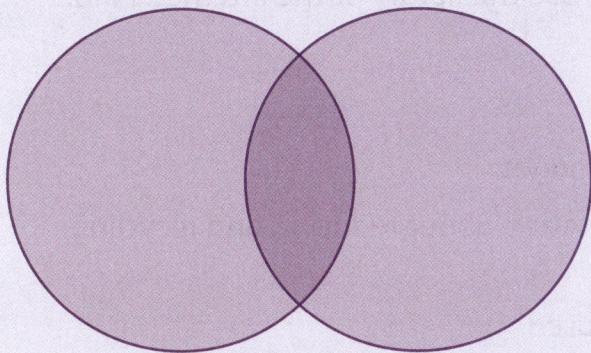

2. Work in small groups. Each group should research a different text type.

    1. Find three examples of your text type.

    2. As a group, discuss your chosen text type and consider the following:
        - language or style used (formal/informal)
        - layout
        - features

    3. Create a poster explaining the characteristics of your text type.

Project 30

Speaking and listening

1. Making plastic bottles causes air pollution, so it is a good idea to use fewer plastic bottles and to recycle the ones that we have. Look at the photograph and discuss these questions.

   1. How are plastic bottles being recycled?
   2. What else can you do with plastic bottles?
   3. What other types of pollution do plastic bottles cause?

2. Work with a partner to research methods to reduce and recycle garbage. You could focus on a specific item, such as plastic bottles or plastic bags. Use the library or the internet. Find:
   - interesting facts
   - data and charts
   - photographs and images.

   Then prepare a presentation about reducing and recycling garbage. Consider:
   - how are the items used
   - why the item is a problem
   - ways to reduce usage
   - ways to recycle the item.

Word builder

Vocabulary box

already	bicycle	electrical	remember
appliances	contribution	exercise	smoke
asthma	cut down	household	solution
atmosphere	deserve	outside	switch off
better	eco-friendly	reduce	

Look and learn

An **antonym** is a word or words that have the opposite meaning.
For example:
happy and *sad*
light and *dark*
night and *day*
big and *small*
old and *new*

A **synonym** is a word or words that have the same meaning.
For example:
happy: delighted, pleased, joyful
light: bright, illuminated
big: huge, large, giant, enormous

1 Find antonyms for the following words.

> increase   forget   switch on   inside   problem   worse

2 Create a list of synonyms for the following words:

- reduce
- clean
- angry
- powerful
- said

Look and learn

Some words are used too often and so they become boring.
For example: *nice, big, very, many, important, lots, go*
Read these sentences. Can you think of any synonyms to use instead?
The smell from the factory is <u>not nice</u>.
Fossil fuels are <u>bad</u> sources of energy.

NOTE:

Make sure that the synonym you choose is appropriate in a sentence.
For example:

Synonyms for **not nice**: unpleasant, unfriendly, ugly, horrible, unkind
The smell from the factory is unpleasant/horrible.
NOT: *The smell from the factory is unfriendly/ugly/unkind.*

3 Work with a partner. Read the story and identify the boring words. Then discuss which synonyms you could use to make the story more interesting. Rewrite the story and read it aloud to your group or class. You can also role-play the story for the class, emphasizing the synonyms you have added to the story.

Last month we went on holiday. We went to a nice place near the beach. We couldn't wait to go and have a swim. We changed into our swimsuits, took off our shoes and went down to the water.

"Ouch!" said my sister. "My foot is sore and bleeding. I walked on some glass."

We had a look around us. There was a lot of litter on the beach; cans and broken glass were lying everywhere.

I picked my sister up and we went home. Mum took her to the clinic. She had stitches in her foot. It was very sore. It was a bad start to the holiday!

Project 30 – Clean air

Let's read

1. Skim this comic story. It doesn't have a title yet, but the pictures give you some clues. Discuss what it is about briefly.

- Tyrone has asthma. We must help him.
- How can we do that?
- We need less air pollution in this house.
- I quit!
- I'll use eco-friendly cleaning products in the house.
- No more burning rubbish. I'll take this to the dump.
- Thanks! And we must stop using cars and buses all the time. I'm going to walk to school.
- And I can take my bicycle to work – it's good exercise too!
- And remember to switch off the lights. Less electricity = less pollution!
- I feel better already.
- Yeah! And we can recycle, too – that also helps.

2 Read the story quietly by yourself and look at the pictures. Discuss and work out the answers to these questions.

1. What is wrong with Tyrone?
2. What can cause this disease?
3. What does father "quit"? Why?
4. Why is it a bad idea to burn rubbish?
5. How does switching off lights and appliances help to reduce air pollution?
6. Why does the family decide to recycle?

3 Now work in groups and give the story a title. Compare your title with other groups' titles.

4 Work with a partner. Plot the story. Complete the table for each part of the story.

Story title:	
Beginning:	
Build up:	
Climax:	
Solving the problem:	
Resolution:	

5 Use your plot table to retell the story to a partner.

> **What's your view?**
> Are there any ways that you could help to reduce air pollution?

Project 30 – Clean air

Grammar builder

Look and learn

We use the **present continuous** tense for an action that is happening right now.

For example: *Tyrone **is** cough**ing**.*

We use the **present simple** tense to describe something that is true now or something that you always do.

For example: *Tyrone has asthma.* (NOT *Tyrone is having asthma.*)

I always switch off the lights when I leave the room.

We use the **past simple** tense for something that has already finished.

I switched off the light as I left the room.

I walked to school.

Remember that some verbs have irregular past tense forms.

He took his bicycle to work.

He quit his job.

1. Draw the table in your notebook and fill in the missing verbs.

Present simple	Present continuous	Past simple
	having	had
walk		walked
	swimming	swam
help		
clean		cleaned
	switching	
go		went
fill		

2. Correct the underlined verbs in the following paragraph.

Mike and Sherwin want to help to cut down on air pollution. "When you <u>burnt</u> plastic bottles, poisonous smoke goes up into the air," explains Mike. So, they <u>are having</u> a new plan. Every day they <u>is going</u> around to the neighbours and <u>collecting</u> plastic bottles. They <u>cleaned</u> the bottles. Then they <u>filling</u> the bottles with sand. They use the bottles to build a wall around their garden.

Term 3 Unit 1

Let's write

Task

Write a story about a family who take action to improve air pollution in their home and community. Use some direct speech in your story.

Plan

1. Discuss your ideas with a partner. Consider the following:
   - Who will be the characters in your story?
   - Why do they decide to take action to improve air pollution?
   - How do they decide to take action to improve air pollution?

2. Draw a table like the one below and fill each section for your story.

Story title:	
Beginning:	
Build up:	
Climax:	
Solving the problem:	
Resolution:	

3. Use your plot table to tell your story to a partner.

Write

4. Follow your plan to draft your story. You could type it on a computer or laptop.

Evaluate

5. Use the "Editor's checklist" to edit your story.

Editor's checklist

- Have you included direct speech in your story, punctuated with quotation marks?
- Did you use paragraphs to structure your story?
- Have you followed your plan?
- Check that the tenses are correct.
- Have you used pronouns to avoid repetition?
- Use synonyms to make you vocabulary more varied for example replace the word said with a more interesting synonym.
- Check that you have spelt homophones correctly.

266

Term 3 Unit 1 Review and assessment

Word builder

1 Give a synonym for the underlined words in each sentence.

    1 Don't throw your <u>rubbish</u> on the street.

    2 The recycled paper is <u>not expensive</u>.

2 Give an antonym for the underlined words in each sentence.

    1 The factory will <u>increase</u> their smoke emissions this year.

    2 The air is <u>clean</u> today!

3 Write your own definitions of these words. Give an example of each word in a sentence.

    1 fuel

    2 pollution

Let's read

1 Read the paragraph and answer the questions.

> Air pollution is a type of pollution that affects most cities. The air in cities is polluted by gas emissions, smoke and smells. Vehicles and factories emit a gas called *carbon monoxide*, which is poisonous and unpleasant. It can make us cough and it can also affect our skin and lungs. Some people burn garbage in towns because their trash is not collected. The smoke from these fires can also affect our health and make our town dirty. The fires also smell bad.

1. Name two causes of air pollution in cities.
2. True or false? Cars emit carbon monoxide.
3. Complete the sentence: Air pollution can affect our …
4. Why is it not a good idea to burn garbage?
5. Give the paragraph a suitable title.

2 Read the poem several times and make notes about the ideas that come to your mind. When you read the poem, pay attention to the punctuation marks rather than the line breaks. Does that help to create a picture in your mind?

Fog

The fog comes
on little cat feet.
It sits looking
over harbour and city
on silent haunches
and then moves on.

by Carl Sandburg

1. What is the poem about? What are the words or phrases that help you to decide?
2. Name the figure of speech used in lines 1 and 2. What does this figure of speech help you to understand about the subject of the poem?
3. What does the poet mean by "silent haunches"?
4. Do you like the title of the poem? Explain your view.

Review and assessment

Grammar builder

1 Rewrite the following story using correct punctuation.

> Yesterday Tyrone and Jo were on their way to the shop. Then Tyrone smelled something.
> "What's that smell?" he asked.
> It smells like a fire, said jo.
> It is a fire! Look at all the smoke! shouted Tyrone.
> What's going on asked Jo.
> I think people are burning their rubbish again! said Tyrone.
> I wish they wouldn't do that said jo.

2 Rewrite the story in the present simple tense.

3 Replace the underlined words with pronouns.

   1 I can smell the fire, but I can't see <u>the fire</u>.

   2 Mike says that <u>Mike</u> feels sick and <u>Mike</u> can't breathe well.

   3 The woman is coughing and sneezing because of the air pollution. Can you help <u>the woman</u>?

Let's write

1 What can you do to make sure that your written work is good? Write down three tips that you could give to others.

2 Write a story. Choose one of the following topics. Use direct speech in your story.

   • We helped to reduce pollution in our town!
   • Pollution is a serious problem.
   • Air pollution is making us sick.

   In your writing, demonstrate that you have planned your paragraphs including a brief introduction and conclusion.